Yorkshire Terriers

Second Edition

by Liz Palika

ALPHA

A member of Penguin Group (USA) Inc.

ALPHA BOOKS

Published by the Penguin Group

Penguin Group (USA) Inc., 375 Hudson Street, New York, New York 10014, USA

Penguin Group (Canada), 90 Eglinton Avenue East, Suite 700, Toronto, Ontario M4P 2Y3, Canada (a division of Pearson Penguin Canada Inc.)

Penguin Books Ltd., 80 Strand, London WC2R 0RL, England

Penguin Ireland, 25 St. Stephen's Green, Dublin 2, Ireland (a division of Penguin Books Ltd.)

Penguin Group (Australia), 250 Camberwell Road, Camberwell, Victoria 3124, Australia (a division of Pearson Australia Group Pty. Ltd.)

Penguin Books India Pvt. Ltd., 11 Community Centre, Panchsheel Park, New Delhi—110 017, India

Penguin Group (NZ), 67 Apollo Drive, Rosedale, North Shore, Auckland 1311, New Zealand (a division of Pearson New Zealand Ltd.)

Penguin Books (South Africa) (Pty.) Ltd., 24 Sturdee Avenue, Rosebank, Johannesburg 2196, South Africa

Penguin Books Ltd., Registered Offices: 80 Strand, London WC2R 0RL, England

International Standard Book Number: 978-1-59257-939-6
Library of Congress Catalog Card Number: 2009924930

11 10 09   8 7 6 5 4 3 2 1

Interpretation of the printing code: The rightmost number of the first series of numbers is the year of the book's printing; the rightmost number of the second series of numbers is the number of the book's printing. For example, a printing code of 09-1 shows that the first printing occurred in 2009.

Printed in the United States of America

Note: This publication contains the opinions and ideas of its author. It is intended to provide helpful and informative material on the subject matter covered. It is sold with the understanding that the author and publisher are not engaged in rendering professional services in the book. If the reader requires personal assistance or advice, a competent professional should be consulted.

The author and publisher specifically disclaim any responsibility for any liability, loss, or risk, personal or otherwise, which is incurred as a consequence, directly or indirectly, of the use and application of any of the contents of this book.

Most Alpha books are available at special quantity discounts for bulk purchases for sales promotions, premiums, fundraising, or educational use. Special books, or book excerpts, can also be created to fit specific needs.

For details, write: Special Markets, Alpha Books, 375 Hudson Street, New York, NY 10014.

Photographs by Sheri Wachtstetter

Publisher: *Marie Butler-Knight*
Editorial Director: *Mike Sanders*
Senior Managing Editor: *Billy Fields*
Acquisitions Editor: *Karyn Gerhard*
Development Editor: *Julie Bess*
Senior Production Editor: *Janette Lynn*

Copy Editor: *Tricia Liebig*
Cover Designer: *Rebecca Harmon*
Book Designer: *Trina Wurst*
Indexer: *Johnna VanHoose Dinse*
Layout: *Ayanna Lacey*
Proofreader: *John Etchison*

Contents at a Glance

Contents

Introduction

This book is not like most other breed books about dogs. Those books are usually written by breeders, dog show judges, or fanciers of the breed. They will tell you in no uncertain terms exactly how wonderful that breed is. You'll see photos of winning show dogs, influential sires, and dogs from years past.

Well, I'm not a Yorkie breeder, nor do I show Yorkies in conformation. This book does not contain any dog show photos, nor do I have photos of influential sires from years past. Instead, I am a Certified Dog Trainer and a Certified Animal Behavior Consultant. I teach dog training classes for dogs and their owners.

I see many Yorkies and their owners; many, unfortunately, are having trouble. Although the owners may have researched the breed prior to adding the Yorkie to their family, once the dog was in the family they began having trouble. Perhaps the dog was having housetraining problems. Or the dog was barking too much.

This book takes a realistic look at Yorkshire Terriers. We'll look at their wonderful characteristics as well as those areas that cause the most trouble. I am a big believer in preventing problems from happening rather than trying to solve the problems once they've occurred, so we'll discuss problem prevention in great detail.

We'll also talk about grooming your Yorkie, feeding him, playing with him, training him, and keeping him healthy. This book has been designed to provide you with all of the information you need to live with and enjoy your Yorkie.

Who Am I?

As I mentioned, I am a dog trainer and behavioral consultant. I have been teaching dogs and their owners for more than 25 years. My business, Kindred Spirits Dog Training, offers classes for puppies as well as basic and intermediate obedience, as well as Canine Good Citizen classes, therapy dog training, trick training, carting, and more.

Although I do believe that dogs need rules for good behavior, I also feel that it's important for you and your dog to have fun with your training.

Decoding the Text

This book is for people who are new to Yorkies or new to dog ownership as well as experienced dog owners. I have avoided technical gibberish and any words that may be in "dog speak," which are defined so there is no confusion.

There are four different sidebars found throughout the book.

Yorkie Smarts

These tips will help make life with a Yorkie easier.

Watch Out!

Pay attention to these boxes. This information is important.

Bet You Didn't Know

This is extra information that you should find helpful.

Dog Talk

These definitions will help you understand the information discussed in the text.

Trademarks

All terms mentioned in this book that are known to be or are suspected of being trademarks or service marks have been appropriately capitalized. Alpha Books and Penguin Group (USA) Inc. cannot attest to the accuracy of this information. Use of a term in this book should not be regarded as affecting the validity of any trademark or service mark.

Part 1

So, You've Got a Yorkie!

Chances are if you've picked up a copy of this book, you're already a fan of Yorkshire Terriers. It's easy to become enamored with this breed—they are small, cute, feisty, and have no idea that they're so tiny. They are always ready to take on the world.

This section is designed to get you started with your Yorkie. We'll talk briefly about where this breed came from, what they are, and the breed's characteristics. However, the most important things you need to do with your dog are to keep him confined and safe. Making your house and yard both safe and escape-proof are very important, and we'll walk you through the process.

Then, we'll talk about what to feed your Yorkie. We'll take a look at commercial foods, homemade foods, and other options. We'll also discuss when to feed your Yorkie, how often, and how much.

Chapter 1

All About Yorkies

In This Chapter

- The attention Yorkies attract
- The origins of the breed
- A quick look at terriers
- A glimpse at what makes Yorkies special

Yorkshire Terriers, usually called "Yorkies," are very attractive and appealing little dogs. Classified as toy breed dogs by the American Kennel Club (AKC) rather than terriers, Yorkies are treasured by both toy dog and terrier enthusiasts.

People who enjoy Yorkies like the breed for a variety of reasons. Some enjoy the breed's tiny size or luscious coat while others enjoy the spunky, rather feisty terrier personality. No matter what appeals to them, people who love Yorkies do so enthusiastically.

Yorkies Are Special

The Yorkshire Terrier is a unique breed of dog. These little bundles of energy are terriers, yet are classified by the American Kennel Club as a toy breed. They are feisty hunters but are also very affectionate. Yorkies are bright and intelligent, yet can also be stubborn and independent. Let's face it, Yorkies are special!

Yorkie Smarts

Yorkies are active dogs from puppyhood through old age. They love to play, hunt, chase, and explore. Wise owners make sure the Yorkie goes out for a good walk every day and has plenty of opportunities to play.

Yorkies also attract attention everywhere they go, although sometimes people can't identify the breed. Comments on the dog's size, beautiful flowing coat, and cuteness are often followed by the question, "What kind of dog is that?" Many times the Yorkshire Terrier is confused with the Silky Terrier, a similar but larger breed.

Tiny Dogs

Yorkies are tiny; usually between five to seven pounds when full grown. Many people treasure this size, but it makes other people uneasy. A tiny dog can be severely hurt or killed if sat or stepped on or inadvertently kicked. Their size makes them more fragile, and everything, including walks and playtimes, must be tailored to their size.

Because of their tiny size, Yorkies are classified by the American Kennel Club as a toy breed dog. Although their name identifies them as a terrier—Yorkshire Terrier—the breed's tiny size sets them apart from other terriers.

Always Affectionate

Yorkies are an affectionate breed. They are loving, demonstrative, and love to cuddle. Unfortunately, this can sometimes get out of hand as some Yorkies spend their life on a lap, and they really do need to get down once in a while!

The breed's affectionate nature has also led them to be very good therapy dogs. Many Yorkies visit hospitals, nursing homes, and senior centers on a regular basis, providing love, affection, and laughter to those people who need it most.

Bet You Didn't Know

Hunting is triggered by movement. If a cat sits still, the Yorkie may approach but will usually do so calmly and quietly. If the cat runs, however, the Yorkie will enthusiastically chase, usually while barking.

Feisty Hunters

Although they are tiny, Yorkies have the heart of a lion. They were originally hunting dogs and retain those instincts. A rat or a mouse (or a butterfly!) is not safe with a Yorkie chasing it.

If given the opportunity, Yorkies will also chase cats, rabbits, and other small pets. Training can help teach the Yorkie that other family pets are not to be harassed.

Protective and Courageous

It may seem ridiculous that a five- to seven-pound dog thinks he's a watchdog, but Yorkies do. They simply don't realize how small they are. Yorkies bark ferociously when someone approaches their yard, house, car, or person. They can't back up that bark with action, of course, but Yorkies don't seem to realize that. I guess they figure their barking will alert backup, and it usually does.

Too much barking, however, can lead to neighbor complaints. All Yorkies should be taught that barking when someone approaches is fine, but the barking should not continue. Early obedience training is a must for all Yorkies.

Attitude Is Everything

Yorkies have a very regal attitude with their head held high, ears up, and coat flowing behind. If you can, go to a *conformation dog* show in your area and watch the Yorkies compete. Attitude is everything!

Dog Talk

In **conformation dog** shows, dogs compete against others of their breed and winners accrue points toward their championship title.

This attitude is what attracts many people to the breed. That "Hey, look at me!" attitude combined with the breed's other attributes can be very appealing. Especially from such a small dog!

Intelligent and Obedient

Yorkies are intelligent—very intelligent—and sometimes, that's a problem. Any dog trainer will tell you that Yorkies are smart, eager to learn, and easy to train. However, Yorkies are also smart enough to figure out alternative ways to do things, so training a Yorkie can also be a challenge. Yorkies are also smart enough to get bored, so training must be innovative and fun.

Yorkies thrive in obedience training, trick training, therapy dog training, canine freestyle, and many other dog sports. Although it's not necessary for every Yorkie to compete or become involved in canine sports—you can train your Yorkie at home if you wish—you may want to check out some dog sports, as they can be great fun.

The Manipulative Yorkie

Okay, this is where Yorkies really excel. Yorkies are very good at manipulating their owners. Those big dark eyes, gorgeous coat, tiny body, and wiggling tail stub can turn any owner into a puddle of mush. Yorkies know how cute they are and how well they are loved, and they use that to their advantage.

Unfortunately, when Yorkies are too manipulative and the owner too soft, the tiny dog can get into too much trouble. A Yorkie who begs for too many treats and is indulged will get fat. A Yorkie who manipulates his owner too much will become too demanding and will lose respect for his owner. Cute is fine, but don't let things get out of hand.

Yorkies are active, agile, intelligent dogs who enjoy many dog sports, including agility.

Energy to Spare

Yorkies are active little dogs. Although they enjoy a snuggle on the sofa, they also like to play games, including ball, and they like to hunt for dust bunnies under the sofa and real bunnies outside. With this energy, Yorkies are great fun and you can invent all kinds of games to play.

However, this energy can also lead to problems. Yorkie puppies may try to chew on your slippers or raid the kitchen trashcan. One thing is for certain, though, sharing your life with a Yorkie will never be boring.

The History of the Breed

The Yorkshire Terrier we know today has a long history. Although the dogs of years past were different from today's Yorkies, those dogs shaped the Yorkshire Terrier we know today.

Small terriers of various kinds and varieties have been common in the British Isles for centuries. Other dogs, especially larger hunting dogs, could only be kept by landowners; the serfs were allowed only small dogs. Landowners enforced this rule because they were afraid that with larger hunting dogs, the serfs would poach game on the landowners' property. So many working people kept small terriers to help control mice and rats.

Dog Talk

Yorkies originated in Scotland and England and the name Yorkshire Terrier comes from Yorkshire, England.

During the Industrial Revolution, people whose families had worked the land for generations flocked to the factories and textile mills to try to better their lives. People from Scotland brought with them small dogs, some known as Clydesdale Terriers and others known as Paisley Terriers. Clydesdale Terriers weighed about 12 pounds and had a silky coat. The Paisley Terriers were about six pounds and were blue and tan.

It is known that these two breeds were crossed to produce a silky-coated ratter; however, few pedigrees were kept, as most of the breeders were illiterate. Verbal histories, passed down through the generations, also spoke of crossings with English Black and Tan Terriers, Toy Terriers, and possibly even Maltese Terriers as well as other unnamed dogs of unknown or mixed breeds.

Eventually the dogs became more uniform in size, coat type, and color. In the mid-1880s, the dogs became known as Broken Haired Scottish Terriers. Then, in 1886, the British Kennel Club recognized these dogs as Yorkshire Terriers.

The Breed's Sire

Hudderfield Ben has been called the *sire* (or father) of the modern Yorkshire Terrier. Owned by M. A. Foster, Ben competed in conformation dog shows, winning frequently. He also competed in rat-killing contests. These were very popular in that era, as were many other blood sports. Born in 1865, Ben was run over by a carriage in 1871, and died in the prime of his life. However, his progeny went on to help establish the breed's popularity in England.

Dog Talk

Sire means father (and **dam** means mother).

The Terrier Personality

The Yorkie's tough, "let me at 'em" personality is a true terrier personality. Most of the small terriers were bred to control vermin and had to have that personality. A small dog with a soft, sensitive temperament would not be as effective a ratter (rats are tough and can have a nasty bite!). Times were tough in that era, too, and often a family might not have enough food to go around. Many times the dog—who was fed table scraps anyway—might have to fend for himself. A hunting terrier could do that.

? Bet You Didn't Know

Rat-killing contests were popular in early England. A dog was put in a pit with a number of rats, and the dog who killed the most rats in the shortest period of time was declared the winner. Because rats were a serious threat to human health, rat-killing dogs were prized.

Popularity Soared

After being recognized by the British Kennel Club, the breed's popularity increased slowly but steadily. During the Victorian era, the wealthier ladies took to this attractive breed and kept them in increasing numbers. Yorkies were used both as a companion and as a ratter in the ladies' rooms.

In the early 1930s, fewer than 500 dogs were registered by the British Kennel Club, but by the mid-1950s more than 2,000 were registered. By the 1970s, the Yorkshire Terrier had become the most popular breed in England. Some of this was due to Ch Blairsville Most Royale, who went Reserve Best in Show at Britain's prestigious Crufts Dog Show, and her son, Ch Blairsville Royal Seal. He won the Ladies Kennel Society dog show in 1976, and then proceeded to win a host of other dog shows for the next two years.

> **? Bet You Didn't Know**
>
> Yorkies were first shown at the Westminster Dog Show in 1878 with 18 in the heavier than 5 pound class and 15 in the less than 5 pound class.

The Yorkie Today

Yorkies have remained very popular, both in the dog show ring and as treasured pets. The Yorkie's attractive appearance is certainly appealing to many people, although numerous pet owners keep that high-maintenance coat trimmed short or even shaved. The breed's tiny size is also a selling point for many people, but there are quite a few small toy breeds. However, when the breed's appearance and size are combined with the terrier spunkiness, well, that seems to create the perfect dog for many people.

Yorkies are very in tune to their people and when not playing are happy to cuddle and snuggle.

Yorkies Are Good Companions

You may have added a Yorkie to your family for many reasons. And if you are looking at this book in anticipation of adding a Yorkie to your life, here are some of the things that Yorkie owners have said about their dogs:

- Your Yorkie will make you laugh, and laughter is always good for you.

- Your Yorkie will warn you of danger by barking fiercely, increasing your sense of security.

- Your Yorkie will attract people's attention, enabling you to meet and talk to other people.

- Your Yorkie needs exercise, and by giving him that exercise, you'll get some, too.

- Your Yorkie needs to play, and play (along with laughter) is good for you.

- Research has shown that people who live with dogs are healthier than people who live alone.

- Your Yorkie is a great listener and wonderful personal therapy.

- Your Yorkie is a great companion. You are never alone when you have a dog.

- Your Yorkie will love you unconditionally with all his heart.

Yorkies Enjoy Dog Sports

Yorkies today are also involved in many dog sports and activities. Although they cannot (because of their small size) compete in some sports, such as Frisbee catch and fetch, or weight-pulling contests, they can still have fun in many other activities, including the following:

- **Agility.** This is a fast-moving, athletic sport where the dog jumps over jumps of different kinds, runs through tunnels, and climbs obstacles, all against a time clock.

- **Conformation dog shows.** Dogs compete against others of their breed to win points toward a breed championship. Winners then compete against other breed winners for Best in Show. For conformation, the Yorkie must be kept in the long, flowing coat.

- **Flyball.** A competitive relay race sport in which dogs run down a path, jump four hurdles, trigger a lever that throws out a tennis ball, and then return the way they came.

- **Therapy dog work.** Trained dogs who like people are evaluated and certified, and then visit people in nursing homes and hospitals as well as schools and daycare centers.

- **Freestyle.** In this sport, dogs and their owners dance to music using dance steps and obedience commands.

- **Competitive obedience.** Dogs and their owners work as a team, completing standard obedience exercises to earn titles.

Although not every dog is a show dog, Yorkie show dog breeders have done a commendable job to keep the breed's appearance as close to the standard as possible. Most Yorkies are still athletes, too, and love to run, jump, and play. Too many Yorkies, however, don't show the bold, courageous temperament the breed should have. Hopefully breeders in the near future will take that into consideration. The breed deserves to carry its head high, as the standard says it should, and be bold and self-confident!

? Bet You Didn't Know

The AKC breed standard for the Yorkshire Terrier is the official written description of the ideal or perfect dog of this breed. Conformation dog show judges look at the dogs competing at each dog show, and compare those dogs to each other and to the standard to choose the best dog competing on that day. You can find the Yorkshire Terrier breed standard by going to the American Kennel Club's website at www.akc.org.

The Least You Need to Know

- The Yorkie was developed as a ratter in England from Scottish and English Terriers.

- Yorkies are wonderful companion dogs for many reasons.

- A Yorkie can be more than just a lap dog; this is a tiny athlete well suited to many dog sports.

- The Yorkie today is a small but bold and self-confident dog.

2

Keeping Your Yorkie Safe

In This Chapter

- ✺ Puppy-proofing your house
- ✺ Puppy-proofing your yard
- ✺ Preventing problems
- ✺ Teaching the "leave it"

Living with a very bright, curious Yorkshire Terrier means you need to keep the safety of your Yorkie in mind. This is especially important when you first bring your Yorkie puppy home. Your Yorkie puppy is an active, busy little being who is curious about everything new, and your house is new to him. But even older puppies and young adults can get into trouble, so keeping him safe will be an ongoing process.

Puppy-proofing your house and yard are the first steps toward keeping your Yorkie safe. You might be amazed at the places a tiny Yorkie can get into. When you make your house and yard safe, you will also be preventing many problem behaviors from occurring. If your Yorkie doesn't learn to raid the trashcan or get into the cat litter box, for example, those behaviors can't turn into bad habits.

Making Your Home Safe for Your Yorkie

Yorkies, both puppies and adults, are curious and can turn just about anything into a toy. Although playing with a paper grocery bag won't hurt your Yorkie and won't cause any more damage than making a mess, chewing on something else—such as plastic—and swallowing a tiny piece could harm your Yorkie and potentially even kill him.

Getting into trouble can also be expensive. Not only may your Yorkie face life-saving surgery should he eat something he shouldn't have, but replacing the television remote control, your cell phone, or your new leather shoes can all add up. If you think your Yorkie is too small to damage your things, think again! Yorkies may be small but they have sturdy jaws.

Young puppies don't realize that chewing on an electrical cord can shock and kill them; they just see this thing dangling in front of their nose that looks like it would be fun to chew on. Because puppies have no common sense and need constant supervision, you need to limit your puppy's freedom and make sure the rooms where he is allowed are safe. We'll talk about limiting his freedom more in this chapter, but first let's talk about how to make your house safe.

Watch Out!

Don't assume a Yorkie will not or cannot chew up something. Yorkie puppies and adolescents are tenacious and stubborn when they want something.

In the rooms where you'll allow the puppy to run around (under your supervision, of course), get down on your hands and knees and look at things from a Yorkie's point of view. Are there magazines that could be chewed up? Pick them up and put them away. Books on the bottom bookshelf? Those are fun to chew. Cords dangling from behind the television, DVD player, and stereo? Remote controls on the sofa end table? Go through the rooms and put away everything valuable, chewable, or dangerous that is within reach.

Here are some things that puppies commonly chew on:

- Electrical cords
- Telephone cords
- Cable and speaker cords
- Remote controls
- Cell and wireless phones
- CDs, DVDs, books, and magazines
- Food, dishes, cups, and utensils
- Shoes and socks
- Children's toys
- Medicine bottles

Impress upon everyone in the house that they need to get into the habit of putting things away, picking stuff up, and closing bedroom or closet doors. When it becomes a habit to do these things, the house becomes much safer for your Yorkie. Make sure, too, everyone understands the new rules. If someone leaves their slippers in the room on the floor and they get chewed up, it's not the Yorkie's fault. He doesn't know any better until he's been taught the rules.

Yorkie Smarts

If you think your Yorkie has eaten something potentially poisonous, the National Poison Control Hotline is 1-800-222-1222 or the ASPCA Animal Poison Control number is 1-888-426-4435.

Dangerous Stuff

Keeping your dog safe means he'll be around longer for you to love and for him to love you. Our homes are full of dangerous things. Make sure all these things are put away and safely out of your puppy's reach.

Some dangerous stuff:

- **Around the house.** Cigarettes (and their ashes and butts), pens and felt tip pens, many different houseplants, laundry products, hobby and craft supplies including glues, and potted plants.

- **In the kitchen.** Oven cleaners, floor cleaners and wax, bug spray, insect and rodent traps, furniture polish, and dishwasher soaps and rinses. Many foods, including candy—especially chocolate.

- **In the bathroom.** Medicines, vitamins, bathroom cleaners, toilet bowl cleaners, some shampoos and conditioners, hair coloring products, and many makeup items. Don't forget the toilet scrub brush.

> **Watch Out!**
> Don't assume your Yorkie will avoid dangerous substances. Instead, assume he will get into them if he can and make sure they're out of reach!

- **In the garage and yard.** Car maintenance products including oils, gas, and antifreeze; fertilizers; weed and insect control products; snail and slug bait; mouse and rat traps and baits; and paints and paint removers. If you have a pool, many of the treatment products are also dangerous. Some landscaping plants are poisonous.

Limit Your Yorkie's Freedom

One of the easiest ways to help protect your Yorkie is to limit his freedom. Dogs have no idea that some things in this world might harm them, so as your Yorkie's protector you need to protect him from himself and his own actions. You can do that by making the house safe as well as limiting his access to those things that could harm him.

Use baby gates to restrict him to one room at a time; preferably the room you're in so you can watch him. When you can't watch him, put him in his kennel crate (we'll talk about that more later) or put him in a child's playpen or exercise pen. An exercise pen is a portable wire fence that works just like a child's playpen; it keeps the puppy confined but gives him enough room to play.

When you limit your Yorkie's freedom, you can prevent him from getting into trouble.

In addition, tiny Yorkie puppies can get into very small spaces. Yorkies can fit beside and behind the refrigerator, under the dishwasher, under the foot of the reclining chair, through a tiny hole in the screen door, and many other dangerous places. When puppy-proofing your house, think small—if a kitten can fit through it—so can a Yorkie!

Searching for Dangers in Your Yard

You need to puppy-proof your yard just as you did your house. Make sure the kids' toys are put away, the gardening supplies are out of reach, all poisonous plants are out of reach (see the list later in this chapter), and the pool chemicals are stored in a safe place. Assume that if anything is left within reach, the puppy will chew on it.

Look at the yard from your Yorkie's point of view; keeping in mind Yorkies are very tiny. Can he get under the deck, and is it dangerous if he does? Is there a place where he can get through the vent under the house? Can he chew on the cords to the lights in the backyard? Does the television cable go into the house inside the yard? Can the Yorkie chew on that cable? There are many things in the backyard that are potentially dangerous or that the puppy can destroy.

Inspect the Fence

Terriers, including Yorkies, are curious. If there's a hole in the fence around your yard, your Yorkie will stick his nose in it. If he can make the hole bigger, he will. He may not want to actually go anywhere, he's just curious about what's on the other side of the fence.

Make sure the fence itself is sound and all holes—even tiny ones—are covered. It may be a good idea to run hardware cloth (wire fencing) over the inside of the fence, from tight to the ground to about three feet high.

Bet You Didn't Know

If you think your fence won't be secure or that your yard has too many dangers, build your Yorkie a dog run. A fenced area that's 4 feet wide by 12 feet long is more than enough.

There should be no holes under the fence, either. If there is a gap between the ground and the fence, a tiny Yorkie can dig enough to get under it.

Do You Need a Dog Run?

I talked about a dog run briefly earlier in this chapter. Yorkies are tiny dogs and can get through some amazingly small holes in a fence. If you have any doubts whatsoever as to whether your Yorkie will be safe in your backyard, build him a dog run. It doesn't have to be huge—a 4 feet wide by 12 feet long run will be fine for your Yorkie for his entire life. Just make it escape proof, with no gaps between the ground and the bottom of the fence.

If you live in an area with birds of prey (hawks or eagles) or other predators such as coyotes, make sure the run has secure fencing over the top, too. When predators are prevalent, I never recommend leaving a small dog outside for long hours at a time; however; the dog run can help keep him safe for short periods of time when the predators are not active.

Look for Dangerous Plants

Many common landscaping plants are dangerous. Some will just make a dog nauseous, but others are toxic. Before allowing your puppy free access to the yard, make sure none of these plants are present.

The plants in the following list are some of the most commonly used landscaping plants that are dangerous for pets; however, if you have any doubts about any plants in your yard or garden, talk to a horticulturist or a poison control center. As the saying goes, "It's always better to be safe than sorry!"

Amaryllis	Buttercup
Avocado (leaves not fruit)	Calla lily
Azalea	Common privet
Belladonna	Crocus
Bird of paradise	Daffodil
Bottlebrush	Dieffenbachia
Boxwood	Dogwood

English ivy

Foxglove

Hemlock

Horse chestnut

Hyacinth

Iris

Jasmine

Lily of the valley

Milkweed

Morning glory

Mushrooms

Oleander

Pennyroyal

Poison ivy, oak, and sumac

Rhododendron

Sweet pea

Tulip

Yew

Is your yard safe for a tiny puppy?

Preventing Problems from Occurring

When you make your home safe for your Yorkie and when you restrict his access to things that could harm him, you are keeping him safe, but you are also preventing him from getting into trouble. When you prevent him from chewing on your shoes, stealing the remote, or raiding the trashcan, you are also preventing problem behaviors from occurring and potentially preventing bad habits from becoming established.

If your Yorkie is in an exercise pen while you're taking a shower, for example, then he can't reach the sofa cushion to chew on it. If he can't chew on the cushion, then he never learns how much fun it is to pull the stuffing out of the cushion. Because dogs will repeat *self-rewarding behaviors*, your dog will never have a chance to learn how much fun this could have been.

Preventing these problems from happening also makes training easier. Your Yorkie should learn that training with you and complying with your wishes is great fun—more fun than chewing on a sofa cushion ever could have been.

You should concentrate on limiting your Yorkie's freedom and watch for potential problems until your Yorkie is mentally mature and his training is well established. For most Yorkies this is between 24 and 30 months of age.

Dog Talk

A **self-rewarding behavior** is something that your dog does and gets pleasure for doing. Raiding the kitchen trashcan is self-rewarding because there are bits of food in there. Your dog will repeat these actions because he likes the reward he derives from it.

Teaching the Leave It

The *Leave It* command teaches your Yorkie that there are certain things you want him to ignore. For example, as has been mentioned previously, Yorkies like to chase small animals, including cats. Chasing cats is a bad habit, especially when most house cats are larger than most Yorkies and have paws full of claws that can damage your Yorkie's eyes! Plus, you don't want your dog to think harassing the family cat is acceptable behavior.

So if you want to teach your Yorkie to leave the family cat alone, put your Yorkie on his leash and hold it. Have a pocket full of really good treats that you know he likes.

- Bring the cat into the room.

- When your Yorkie moves toward the cat, tell him, "Sweetie, leave it!"

- Using the leash, turn your dog toward you, let him sniff the treat, and tell him *Watch Me* as you bring the treat toward your face.

- When he looks at you—even if he's watching the treat, too— praise him, "Good boy to watch me!"

- If he's fighting the leash to chase the cat, take hold of his collar, turn him away from the cat as you say "leave it," and repeat the Watch Me exercise.

This will be easy if your Yorkie is motivated by treats and more difficult if your Yorkie really likes to chase the cat. But all dogs can learn it so just keep practicing.

Dog Talk

Leave it means ignore what you're paying attention to when I say "leave it."

Watch me means look at me.

Teach Leave It with other things, including other dogs out on your walk, kids dashing past on their skateboards, and food that you drop to the floor. You can even tell your Yorkie "leave it" when he's tugging on your pant legs as you're trying to walk.

Use the Watch Me whenever you need your dog's attention. If you want him to sit and he's excited about something, tell him "watch me" and then "sit." In the beginning, of course, always have him on leash and have a treat in hand so that he doesn't ignore you. But we'll discuss training in more detail in Part 3 of this book.

Take Time to Enjoy Your Yorkie

This chapter is pretty serious; we talked about how to keep your Yorkie safe, how to prevent your dog from getting into trouble, and why restricting his freedom is so vital to his safety. These are all necessary parts of dog ownership and so they are all important.

However, make sure you take the time to enjoy your Yorkie, too. Yorkie puppies are so tiny and so endearing, and they grow up so very fast. Watch your Yorkie as he plays, as he discovers how his legs work, and as he investigates the world around him.

If your Yorkie is a little older, he's still fun to watch. Encourage him as he looks for bugs in the leaf litter in your backyard and enjoy his terrier instincts when he tries to chase a rabbit. Play games with him, throw the ball, and enjoy snuggling with him later when you're both tired. Take the time to enjoy your little dog.

The Least You Need to Know

- ⋈ Take a look at your house from your Yorkie's point of view to make sure there is nothing dangerous your dog can chew on, eat, or steal.

- ⋈ Yorkies can get into trouble easily so make sure your yard, including the fence, is secure and safe.

- ⋈ Limit your dog's freedom until he is mentally mature and very well trained.

- ⋈ The "leave it" teaches your dog to ignore certain things on your command, including cats.

Chapter 3

Feeding Your Yorkie

In This Chapter

- ✄ What to know about commercial dog foods
- ✄ What the scoop is on home-cooked and raw foods
- ✄ How to study supplements
- ✄ When to feed and how much

News reports bombard us daily with information about what foods are good for us and what foods are horrible. One week we may hear that a certain food will prevent cancer and the next week another report will say how unhealthy that same food is. When it's so hard to keep track of the foods we should eat, how can we figure out what our dogs should eat?

Luckily, feeding our dogs is a little easier; their natural diet is a little simpler than ours is. However, we still need to find out as much as we can about our dogs' nutritional needs so that we can provide them with the best diet possible for good health.

All About Canine Nutrition

Dogs are *carnivores*, just as their ancient ancestors and distant cousins, wolves, are. Carnivores eat meat, both by catching prey and by taking advantage of carrion (already dead prey). Very often, their prey was an *herbivore*. Wolves in the far north, for example, hunt caribou. However, when meat is unavailable (perhaps a hunt failed) almost all canine carnivores are also known to eat fallen fruits, berries, and some tubers and roots. Although this might seem to make canines *omnivores*—animals that eat meats and plants—they are still officially classified as carnivores.

Dog Talk

An **herbivore** eats plants; a **carnivore** eats meat; and an **omnivore** eats plants and meat.

Your Yorkie needs a diet that supplies all his nutritional needs. Good nutrition helps his body function as it should, maintains his health, and allows him to grow. The foods he eats also supply him with energy for exercise and play.

Good nutrition is made up of many things. Vitamins, minerals, proteins, amino acids, enzymes, fats, and carbohydrates are all necessary parts of your dog's daily diet:

- ✂ **Vitamins.** These organic compounds are necessary for life. Without them, food could not be digested, your dog could not grow, and there would be a total cessation of a thousand other bodily functions. Several vitamins, including A, D, E, and K, are fat soluble, which means the body can store them in fat. Other vitamins, including all the B complex vitamins and C, are water soluble. These are flushed out of the system daily in the urine and must be replenished through the foods consumed.

Yorkie Smarts

If you find your Yorkie eating dirt or chewing on rocks, he may be suffering from a mineral deficiency. Offer him a daily mineral supplement.

❧ **Minerals.** These inorganic compounds are also necessary for life, although in much smaller amounts than vitamins. Necessary minerals include calcium, phosphorus, copper, iron, and potassium, as well as several others. Minerals require a delicate balance for good health—some work only in the presence of others.

❧ **Protein.** Meat is good-quality protein; beef, chicken, lamb, fish, or any other meat. Proteins are found in other sources, too, including eggs, dairy products, and some plants. Complete proteins contain all the amino acids necessary for good health. Incomplete proteins contain some, but not all, of the necessary amino acids. Good sources of complete proteins include eggs, red meats, fish, milk, and dairy products. Incomplete proteins, which are still good nutrition when combined with other proteins, include beans, peas, soybeans, peanuts, grains, and potatoes.

> **? Bet You Didn't Know**
>
> The amino acids essential for canine life include arginine, citrulline, histidine, isoleucine, leucine, lysine, methionine, phenylalanine, taurine, threonine, tryptophan, and valine.

❧ **Amino acids.** Amino acids are necessary for many body functions including growth and healing as well as for hormone, antibody, and enzyme production. When proteins are digested, they are broken down into amino acids, making them usable by the body. There are 22 known amino acids, and 12 of those are considered essential for canine life.

❧ **Enzymes.** Enzymes are protein-based chemicals that cause biochemical reactions in the body and affect every stage of metabolism (the process of converting food to its chemical parts, which can then be used by the body). Some enzymes must work with a partner, a coenzyme that is often a vitamin or a mineral, to cause the needed reaction or metabolism. Some enzymes are produced in the dog's body while others are found in the food the dog eats.

- **Fats.** Fats are a necessary part of good nutrition, especially for growing puppies and active dogs. Fats are needed to metabolize the fat-soluble vitamins and to supply energy for activity. Fats may be found in animal meats and in plant-based oils.

Bet You Didn't Know

Some dogs who are fed foods high in carbohydrates (especially carbohydrates from cereal grains) will show symptoms of hyperactivity. These symptoms often disappear when the dog is fed a food lower in cereal grain carbohydrates.

- **Carbohydrates.** Carbohydrates are sugars and starches found in plants. Carbohydrates are fuel for the body. Your Yorkie's body runs on carbohydrates similar to your car running on gasoline. Complex carbohydrates (potatoes, pasta, peas, grains, and rice) are intricate conglomerations of glucose (sugar) molecules.

Commercial Dog Foods

Commercial dog foods were the original convenience food; they were introduced to help dog owners feed their pets more easily. The first commercial dog foods were not based on the science of canine nutrition, but rather on the availability of ingredients. They often contained horse or mule meat, wheat or corn.

Most modern dog food companies, especially the larger ones, have research departments and produce dog foods that are designed to supply all your Yorkie's needs, including proteins, amino acids, enzymes, fats, carbohydrates, vitamins, and minerals. However, all commercial dog foods are not created equal.

What makes one dog food better than another can be based on many things. How and whether the food is tested during development can be used in considering if it's a quality product. Testing may consist of *feeding trials* and, in fact, many of the larger companies, Iams for example, maintain large kennels for feeding trials. In some feeding trial kennels, generations of dogs have been fed only those specific diets while other feeding trials may last only six weeks.

But feeding trials are not the only means of testing the foods; some companies use laboratory testing to determine the nutritional value of a food. However, laboratory testing doesn't necessarily prove that a dog will thrive on the food. Foods that are tested by actually feeding dogs (feeding trials) will say so on the label of the dog food, or you can call the company that makes the food. There should be a phone number on the label.

Dog Talk

Feeding trials are tests in which certain numbers of dogs in a controlled environment, such as a kennel, are fed a specific food for a specific period of time. The dogs' health is analyzed during and after the trials.

Melamine (a mildly toxic substance used in making furniture and other products) was added to pet food ingredients in China to boost the protein levels of the ingredients in laboratory tests. This illegal additive caused many of the pet food recalls that made the news in 2006 and 2007.

The quality of a dog food is also based on the quality of the ingredients. Grains grown in mineral-poor soils will have few minerals to pass on to the dog who consumes them. Poor-quality meats will be less nourishing for the dog. Less-expensive foods typically contain inexpensive and less-nourishing grains and less of the more expensive, but more nutritionally satisfying, meats. Again, the dog's nutrition can, and often will, suffer when he is fed low-quality foods.

Many dog owners are also concerned about many of the preservatives, artificial flavorings, and additives in a lot of dog foods. Some of these additives are of questionable nutritional value. If you are concerned about a particular additive or ingredient, call your veterinarian and call the manufacturer of the food. Find out what they say about that ingredient.

> **? Bet You Didn't Know**
>
> Yorkies suffering from poor nutrition will have a dry or dull coat, flaky skin, brittle nails, and will be more lethargic than normal.

Reading the Label

The label on each bag (or can) of dog food will tell you a lot about that particular food. One section of the label lists the percentages of nutrients. Most Yorkies will thrive on a food that contains about 28 percent protein and 8 percent fat, although if your Yorkie is older and tends to gain weight, a slightly lower percentage of fat is fine.

The label will also tell you the ingredients of the food. Ingredients are listed in order of amounts contained. Therefore, if beef is listed first, followed by rice, corn, and wheat, you'll know there is more beef in the food than there is rice and there is more rice than corn. This can be deceptive, though. For example, if you have a dog food label that lists the ingredients like this: beef, wheat bran, wheat germ, and wheat middlings; does that mean there is more beef than wheat? No, it doesn't. It means only that there is more beef than wheat bran; and more beef than wheat germ. However, if all the wheat ingredients were added together, there is probably much more wheat than beef.

> **Yorkie Smarts**
>
> Although Yorkies aren't as prone to major allergies as are some other toy or terrier breeds, some suffer from food allergies. If you have an allergic Yorkie, reading the ingredients on the dog food label is very important.

The foods listed on the dog food labels may have different definitions than you are used to, as well. Here are some definitions as determined by the Association of American Feed Control Officials, one of several organizations that govern pet foods.

- **Beef:** When a meat is listed by the species name, such as beef, that means that muscle meat from cattle is being used, as well as some organ meats, the tongue, and it may or may not include fat, skin, sinews, nerves, and so on. The same applies to other meats. Because this generally contains primarily muscle meat and organs, the quality is generally very good.

- **Beef by-products:** By-products applies to those parts that are not muscle meats and may include organs, such as lungs, spleen, and kidneys, as well as blood, bone, and fatty tissues. Because the organs and other ingredients can vary tremendously from batch to batch, the quality of by-products can vary from very good to horrible.

- **Beef meal:** Meat meals are made from parts of the beef that are not used in by-products or meats; the definition says, "exclusive of any blood, hair, hoof, hide trimmings, manure, stomach and rumen contents, *except* in such amounts as may occur unavoidably in good processing standards."

- **Barley:** Consists of at least 80 percent barley and must not contain more than 3 percent heat-damaged kernels, 6 percent foreign material, 20 percent other grains, or 10 percent wild oats.

To see more definitions, do an Internet search for the Association of American Feed Control Officials and take a look at their complete list of pet food ingredient definitions.

Are Preservatives Safe?

Preservatives are added to commercial dog food to keep it from spoiling. Unfortunately, not all preservatives are created equal. The most controversial preservative currently used in dog foods is ethoxyquin, a chemical that prevents the fats in foods from becoming rancid and the vitamins from losing their potency. Ethoxyquin is approved by the Food and Drug Administration for use in human foods, but it has come under criticism from the general public. It has been alleged that ethoxyquin causes cancer and kidney, liver, and thyroid problems. However, none of these claims have been proven.

If you are concerned about ethoxyquin or any other chemical preservatives, look for a food preserved with tocopherols. These antioxidants are naturally occurring compounds of vitamins C and E. Just be aware that tocopherols have a very short shelf life; make sure to check the expiration date on the food.

Different Forms of Food

Dog foods are found in four basic forms: dry kibble, canned, semi-moist, and fresh foods (which may also be frozen):

- ✍ Dry, kibbled foods come in a bag and usually contain grains and meats. Dry foods have a good shelf life, and most dogs eat them quite readily. They are usually very affordable; some more so than others. However, the high temperatures needed to process the food can kill or damage many of the beneficial aspects of the food, including vitamins.

- ✍ Canned foods are mostly meats (chunks or slices of meats) or meat recipes (processed meats with other ingredients). These foods have a high moisture content; sometimes as much as 78 to 85 percent. In the can they have a long shelf life, but after the can is opened they must be used right away. Canned foods are very palatable to dogs but are much more expensive than dry foods.

- ✍ Semi-moist foods have a higher moisture content than dry kibble foods but not as high as canned foods. These foods are very high in sugar and salt as well as artificial colorings. The ingredients can also vary significantly, so it's even more important to read the label carefully. Many treats are semi-moist in formulation. Most of these foods should be considered junk food.

🦴 Fresh foods have become quite popular in the past few years. These foods are usually meat recipes (meats combined with other ingredients, usually vegetables but not cereals). Fresh foods are very difficult to preserve without adding preservatives; the shelf life is a matter of days. Therefore, most of these foods are preserved by freezing, although some are dehydrated.

🦴 Some dog owners prefer to feed human food to their dogs, cooking for them on a daily basis, while others have decided to feed a diet based on raw (uncooked) foods. Both of these can work well for your Yorkie as long as you follow a well-balanced recipe or diet.

> **? Bet You Didn't Know**
>
> Nutrition is a very complex subject, and I could write a book on reading the labels and selecting the right food for your dog. In fact, I did! It's called *The Ultimate Pet Food Guide* (DaCapo, 2008).

Cooking for Your Yorkie

I cooked for one of my dogs. I began doing this years ago when one of my dogs had liver disease. She lived to be an old dog and thrived on my home cooking, so I continued to cook for all my dogs.

Cooking for your dog can be a lot of work, though. It is certainly more work than scooping some dry kibble out of the bag! But cooking for your dog requires thought, too, because it can be quite difficult to formulate a home-cooked diet that meets all your dog's nutritional needs. Yorkies present a special challenge, too, because they are so tiny. With a stomach the size of a small walnut, Yorkies get full very quickly. You have to make sure they get all the nutrition they need in that walnut-size meal!

The key to making a homemade diet work is using a variety of ingredients to make sure the dog is receiving all the necessary amino acids and enzymes, as well as his required vitamins and minerals.

The following recipe is a home-cooked maintenance diet for dogs with no known food allergies. The amount fed each day will vary depending on your Yorkie's weight, weight loss or weight gain, activity level, and energy needs. Most Yorkies should be offered approximately ⅓ to ½ cup of the finished food per meal (figuring on two meals per day). Increase or decrease it from there as your dog loses or gains weight.

Mix well together in a big bowl:

1 lb. cooked ground meat (chicken, turkey, or lamb) drained of most fat

½ cup flaxseed meal, finely ground

½ cup sweet potato, cooked, mashed

¼ cup carrots, finely grated, steamed

¼ cup greens, finely chopped (broccoli, romaine lettuce, or other greens), steamed

2 TB. olive oil

Divide into meal-size servings (usually ⅓ to ½ cup) and store in the freezer. Thaw one day's serving at a time.

When serving, add the following:

1 tsp. yogurt with live active cultures

1 multi-vitamin/mineral dog *supplement*

Tiny pinch of kelp

Yorkie Smarts

A **supplement** is anything that is added to the dog's diet. It may be a commercial supplement, an herbal remedy, or other foods.

Your Yorkie doesn't eat much food (he has a tiny tummy!), so the food he eats should be of excellent quality.

Choosing the Right Food

What kind of food should you feed your Yorkie? Because Yorkies eat so little—especially when compared to larger dogs—the choice of what to feed them is very important. Here are some suggestions to help you choose the right food for your Yorkie:

- Tiny dogs sometimes have trouble chewing dry kibble. Is that a problem? If it is, you need to crush the kibble, soak it to soften it, or feed him softer foods.

- Take a good look at the list of ingredients on the dog food label. Do you understand what the ingredients are? Are you comfortable with your dog eating those ingredients?

- What are the protein and fat percentages? Most Yorkies thrive on a diet of at least 28 percent protein and 8 percent fat.

🦴 How active is your Yorkie? If you are training for competitive obedience and agility, you may need to feed him a food higher in calories.

🦴 If you have any questions about the food, talk to your veterinarian and call the food manufacturer.

After your dog has been eating the food for four to six weeks, evaluate the results. This is the food's final test, and will help you decide whether you have chosen the right food for your dog. Answer the following questions:

🦴 How is your dog's weight? Is he too skinny? Is he too fat? You should be able to feel ribs (with a little flesh over them) but not see them.

🦴 How is your Yorkie's coat? It should be shiny and soft with no oily feel and no doggy odor.

🦴 What is your Yorkie's energy level like? Does he have enough energy for work and play? Does he have too much energy? Does he seem hyperactive? He should have plenty of energy for work and play without bouncing off the walls!

🦴 Does he act starved or always hungry? Often dogs whose bodies are missing vital nutrients will chew on everything and will act starved even though they are eating regularly.

Taking a Look at Supplements

Do you take vitamins? You probably feel better about your own overall diet and nutritional health when you do. For the same reason, many dog owners feel better about their dog's nutritional well-being when they add a vitamin/mineral supplement to the diet.

Supplements don't have to be in pill form, however. A supplement is anything that is added to the basic diet, and that can include some herbal remedies as well as foods with special nutritional qualities.

A supplement can make the difference between good nutrition and better nutrition.

Some supplements that can add to your Yorkie's better nutrition and that will not cause a nutritional imbalance might include the following:

- **Yogurt.** A good nutritious food on its own and a good source of protein, amino acids, and fat. Yogurt with live active cultures adds beneficial bacteria to the digestive tract. Add no more than one teaspoon per day for a Yorkie.

- **Brewer's yeast.** Excellent source of B vitamins and minerals, including the essential trace minerals chromium and selenium; a good nutritious food on its own. A dash or a pinch per meal is fine for Yorkies.

> **Watch Out!**
> Too much supplementation can upset the nutritional balance of the previously balanced commercial food. Supplement carefully and wisely. When in doubt, talk to your veterinarian, the dog food company, and the makers of the supplement, and then balance all their recommendations.

- **Eggs.** Cooked only (raw egg yolks interfere with vitamin B absorption and have been associated with salmonella poisoning) are excellent sources of proteins, a variety of vitamins, minerals, and amino acids. Cook one egg and split it up between several meals.

- **Kelp.** A good source of iodine, calcium, potassium, and other minerals and essential trace elements. Use according to manufacturer's directions; usually a pinch is plenty.

When adding supplements to your Yorkie's food, make sure you add small amounts so that the total supplements do not add up to more than 10 percent of the dog's daily diet. Any more than this could upset the nutritional balance of the commercial food.

When, Where, and How Much to Feed

Tiny Yorkie puppies should eat at least twice per day, although offering three meals per day is also fine. Very small puppies can develop hypoglycemia (low blood sugar) if their meals are spread too far apart.

Adult Yorkies will do well with two meals per day, in the morning and evening.

Do Not Free-Feed Your Yorkie

Although it may seem easier to leave a bowl of food out all the time, don't do this. First of all, food left out all the time will easily spoil. If you're feeding homemade cooked food, raw food, or even canned food, bacteria could build up and make your Yorkie sick. Even a dry kibble food could spoil if ants or flies get into it.

In addition, should your dog not feel good one day, the first thing your veterinarian will ask is, "How is your dog's appetite?" If your dog picks at his food all day long, you won't be able to answer that question.

Last but certainly not least, it's important that your dog understand that all his food comes from you. Psychologically, knowing that you are the giver of the food is important.

Where to Feed

Feed your Yorkie in a quiet place where he won't be disturbed. You might want to feed him in his crate, with the door closed, and the crate located in either your bedroom or a quiet part of the family room. Or he can eat in a quiet corner of the kitchen.

Find a spot that will work and then regularly feed your dog there. Don't keep moving his spot from here to there; dogs like routine—especially regarding their food—and changes will upset him.

Obesity can be a problem in this breed, so limit treats and make sure your dog gets a chance to get some exercise every day.

Don't let people mess with him while he's eating, either. Don't reach into his bowl and mess with his food while he's eating and don't put his food down and then take it away again. Unfortunately, information from otherwise well-meaning people has been written that says to prevent your dog from guarding his food reach into his bowl, mess with his food, and take it away from him while he's eating. Let's use common sense, folks. If you give me my food and then mess with it like that, I'm going to start growling myself! I'm going to get downright grumpy and may begin guarding the food even if I had no intentions of guarding it previously.

Now, if you think your dog has the ability or intention to guard his food, hand feed him a third to half of his meal before you set his bowl down; that way he knows it's coming from you. He also knows that you're giving it to him. But after you put the bowl down, let him eat in peace.

Yorkies Don't Eat Much!

Your Yorkie docs not need much food. As you saw in the section on home-cooked meals, ⅓ to ½ cup is a large Yorkie-size serving of food. Many Yorkies will need even less. With any food—commercial dry kibble, canned food, or even a home-cooked diet—you can tell how much to feed by watching your Yorkie. If he gains extra weight, cut back a little on the amount you're feeding him. If he begins to lose weight when he shouldn't, feed him a little more.

Although commercial dog foods will state on the label how much food you should feed your dog, it is simply a guideline. All dogs—even those of the same breed—have individual needs. One dog could eat ⅓ cup, maintain his weight well, and have plenty of energy while another gains weight on the same amount.

Obesity Is a Problem

I'm not trying to be funny when I say obesity is a growing problem today. Far too many Yorkies are fatter than they should be, and this is a definite threat to their health, quality of life, and potential longevity.

Fat Yorkies can suffer from the same health problems that fat people suffer from, including strains on the joints and the organs (including the heart), and increased risk of diabetes.

A Yorkie at a good weight will have a definite waistline. When looking at him from above, his waist will tuck in slightly before the hips. When looking at him from the side, his tummy will tuck up slightly between the ribs and hips. His ribs will have meat over them, but not much.

You don't need to feed your Yorkie a special food for him to lose weight; just cut down the amount of food he's getting, offer low-fat treats (such as bits of raw carrot or apple), and increase his exercise.

The Least You Need to Know

- Dog food labels will tell you a lot about the food, including ingredients, nutritional value, and the preservatives used.

- Dog food labels will not tell you anything about the quality of the ingredients or the digestibility of the foods.

- Healthy homemade diets are possible; but take care with your ingredients and watch your dog closely to monitor the results.

- Most Yorkies will do well when fed twice a day, although puppies may need to eat more often.

Part 2

You Are Your Yorkie's Parent

Although your first reaction may be to deny that you are in any way the parent to a dog, this is actually the best way to describe the relationship you should have with this cute little bundle of wiggles and kisses.

The best parents are leaders; they are fair, firm, and affectionate leaders because puppies and young dogs need leadership. They need a parent to teach them what the world is like and what their place in the world is. In this section, we talk about your responsibilities as a parent.

We also discuss canine communication and learning. Training is often a confusing subject that many dog owners would rather ignore, but it doesn't have to be that way. When you know how to communicate with your dog and learn to understand what he's trying to tell you, training can be fun. In this section we introduce some household rules, housetraining, and how to teach your Yorkie not to bite, and we finish up by discussing the importance of socialization.

Chapter 4

Be a Parent Now and Best Friends Later

In This Chapter

- Discovering the importance of parenthood
- Learning to be your Yorkie's parent
- Learning important leadership skills
- Letting your Yorkie be your best friend later

You probably added a Yorkie to your family because you wanted a cuddly canine companion. You wanted a dog to walk, a dog to play with, and a dog that would bark when strangers appear. Plus, the most common reason why people add a dog to their life is that they're looking for a canine best friend. There is nothing like the relationship people have with their dogs.

Your new Yorkie will be able to be your best friend but that's going to happen later, when your Yorkie is well-trained, well-behaved, and mentally mature. Right now, as a puppy or a young dog, he needs your leadership and guidance. Right now he needs a parent.

Your Yorkie Needs a Parent First

In a natural situation, wolf cubs, coyote pups, or other wild canine pups will remain with their mother for several months, sometimes even a year or two. Mom teaches the pups the rules of canine behavior, how to hunt, and how to survive in a potentially harsh world.

Yorkie Smarts

The definition of a good parent (for children) says that the person assuming the role of a parent must provide not just adequate physical care for the child but also an atmosphere of good emotional mental health. A parent teaches skills for the child's future adult life.

We take domestic puppies away from their mother at 8 to 10 weeks of age—a much younger age than would ever happen in the natural world—and so Mom gets to teach them very little before they join the world of people. So even if you had added a dog to your family because you wanted a new best friend, this puppy needs an adoptive mother first.

As an adoptive mother (or father), you need to teach your Yorkie many things, including …

- **Where to sleep.** Ideally your Yorkie will be sleeping in his crate in your room. We'll talk about this in more detail in upcoming chapters.

- **Where to eat.** Ideally, your Yorkie needs a quiet place to eat where he won't be disturbed. He can eat in his crate or a quiet corner of the kitchen. This was talked about in more detail in Chapter 3.

- **Not to bite people.** Puppies bite each other; they don't have hands and so manipulate the world with their teeth. In Chapter 8, we talk about teaching "no bite" in more detail.

Although your Yorkie may grow up to become your best friend, right now he needs you to act like his parent.

> **Where to relieve himself.** The puppy has the instincts to move away from his bed or den when he needs to relieve himself, so where should he go? As is discussed in Chapter 7, you need to walk him to the place where you want him to go.

> **What the rules of the home are.** Where can he go? Where should he not go? What's safe to touch? What's dangerous? The parent will teach the puppy all these things. You'll learn how to establish these rules in Chapter 6.

? **Bet You Didn't Know**

A mother dog who was taught social rules by her mother will pass them down to her puppies. However, a mother dog who was not taught by her Mom will be unable to teach her pups because she wasn't taught how.

Teach Respect

One of the most important lessons your Yorkie needs to learn is that he must treat you—and other people—with the same respect his mother demanded of him. He is not allowed to treat you as he did his littermates—jumping on them, biting them, grabbing and shaking them, stealing toys, stealing food, and all those other disrespectful things that puppies do to each other. Instead, he needs to treat you with the same respect he showed his mother.

Should he treat you disrespectfully, stop him. Grab his collar or the scruff of his neck and simply stop him as you say in a deep, gruff tone of voice, "No! That's enough!" The deep tone of voice is somewhat of a mimic of his mother's voice when she growled at him when he was bad.

If your Yorkie stops the bad behavior when you interrupt it, let go of him, don't say anything else, and let him think about it for a few moments. After a few moments, hand him a toy and encourage him to play with the toy. He can bite that, growl at it, shake it, and do all those things he tried to do to you. Praise him when he's playing with the toy.

If he doesn't stop the bad behavior and continues to attack you (even in play), then grab his collar or scruff of the neck again, tell him, 'No!" firmly again, and take him to his crate. Put him in the crate for 15 minutes. Don't let him out if he's throwing a temper tantrum, crying, screaming, or biting at the crate; let him out when he's calm and quiet.

Bet You Didn't Know

When crate training your Yorkie, it's important not to punish your dog in the crate. Using the crate for a timeout, as is suggested here, is not a punishment because you are not standing outside the crate yelling at your dog; you put him in there to stop unwanted behavior and to give him a chance to calm down.

Teach Your Yorkie About Love

The most successful parents, those whose children grow up to be happy, healthy adults themselves, have learned to create a home where the children know that they are loved yet also know there are limits to their behavior.

If you can create this same situation for your Yorkie, then your chances of raising a well-behaved dog will be increased. But let's talk about this for a minute, because both parts of this are important. Your Yorkie needs to know he is loved, yet he also needs to know there are limits to his behavior.

When you love your dog, you will smile when you see him. You'll talk to him in a friendly voice and will praise him when he does things right. You will pet him, touch him gently, feed him the best foods you can, make sure he gets the veterinary care he needs, and learn as much as you can about caring for him. You will buy books like this one!

However, loving your dog does not translate into spoiling him. A spoiled dog who has never been taught that there are limits to his behavior will not be fun to live with. He will demand what he wants by barking, jumping, clawing, and sometimes even biting. He will treat you and other people with disrespect. He may lift his leg to urinate on things that belong to you or other people and he may mount (hump) inanimate objects or even your leg. A spoiled dog is a brat, and potentially, even a dangerous dog.

A Good Parent Is a Good Leader

What have good leadership skills got to do with being a good parent? Good *leaders* are usually good parents and vice versa. After all, parenting is more than making breakfast in the morning or cleaning up messes; it is also guiding the young in the direction you want them to grow up. That's leadership!

Dog Talk

A **leader** is one who can guide other people; one who can direct or influence others' actions.

People have a tendency to think of good leaders as people who are gruff, rough, and bossy. John Wayne may come to mind. Good leaders, however, do not have to be rough and gruff. There are as many different ways to be a leader as there are people, and with practice, you will develop your own style of leadership.

However, in regard to your Yorkie, here are some leadership skills that can help you become a better parent:

- Teach your Yorkie what you want him to do and then reward him (with verbal praise, treats, or a toy) for doing it.

- Interrupt bad behavior by stopping it when you catch your dog in the act but never punish your dog when you find a problem later. Corrections after the fact never work.

- When your dog does something right on his own (chooses to play with his toy instead of your shoe), praise and reward him for making the right choice!

- A tired dog is a happy dog; make sure he gets good vigorous exercise each and every day.

- Use a portion of your dog's food each day as training rewards.

- Be calm. Don't get excited, scream or holler, or dance around the room when you're angry. Worse yet, never hit or kick. Instead, be calm and controlled.

Teaching the Sit Command

All the basic obedience commands that you will eventually teach your Yorkie are important. However, the Sit is the first command you will teach your Yorkie and one of the easiest to teach in regard to establishing your leadership skills.

Dog Talk

Sit means lowering the hips to the ground, keeping the front end up, and holding still.

Teaching your Yorkie to sit using the *Sit* command is relatively easy. Teaching him to sit still is a little harder, but we'll take this in small steps and set him up to succeed.

As you begin training your Yorkie, you will be teaching him more than just obedience commands; you will also be teaching him the rules of correct social behavior.

With the leash hooked to your Yorkie's collar, lift him up on his grooming table or a chair. You want to be close to him at this point in training.

Hold his leash or collar in one hand so he doesn't jump off the table or chair, and have a treat in the other hand. Show him the treat and let him sniff it. When he reaches up to sniff the treat, move it over his head toward his tail as you tell him, "Sweetie pie, sit." When his head comes up and back to follow the treat, his hips will go down. After he sits, praise him and give him the treat.

If he spins around to try to get the treat rather than sitting, put the treat in your pocket. Put one hand on his chest where the chest and neck meet. Tell him "Sweetie pie, sit," and at the same time, push that hand slightly up and back (thereby pushing his chest up and back) as the other hand slides down his back toward the hips and tucks his hips down and under. Think of a teeter-totter; up and back at the chest and down and under at the hips. When he's sitting, praise him.

We want your Yorkie to understand that the word "sit" means "put your hips on the ground, keeping your front end up, and be still." Now, obviously, you can't tell your Yorkie this and expect him to understand, so you must teach him that is what it means, and you can do this using your voice. When he does sit, praise him with a higher than normal tone of voice, "Good boy to sit!" When he begins to move from position (not after he's gone) but as soon as he begins to move, use your growling tone of voice, "Acckk!" and put him back in the sit position.

When you are ready for him to move (after a few seconds) tell your dog, "Okay!" and using the leash, gently pull him out of the sitting position. Praise him. The okay is your dog's Release command, the command that tells him he's done with that exercise for the moment.

The Sit is a very useful command, not just as the foundation command for more advanced commands, but also for use around the house, as in the following situations:

- Have your Yorkie sit to greet people, especially if he likes to scratch their legs. He can't jump on people and sit at the same time.

- Have him sit when you hook up his leash to take him outside. If he's sitting, he can't be spinning around in circles out of excitement.

- When he wants you to play with him, have him sit first. Have him sit each time you go to throw his ball or toy.

- Have him sit as you fix each meal and make sure he's sitting before you put his bowl on the floor. When he sits, he won't be clawing your legs or trying to jump up and knock the bowl out of your hands.

- Have him sit at every doorway and give him permission before he goes through. This gives you control of access to the house (or out of the house); both of which are important.

After several days of practice, when your Yorkie is sitting each time you ask him to, you can move him to the floor. Stand up with a treat in hand, and ask him to sit. When he sits, praise him.

Becoming Your Best Friend

As I write these words, Bashir, my 4-year-old canine best friend, is lying under the desk with his head on one of my feet. I'm careful not to even twitch that foot because I don't want to disturb him. Whenever I'm writing, Bashir is right there. When it's time for a break—once an hour or so—he gets up, stretches, and reminds me that time has passed. We go outside, get a drink and maybe a snack, and after a few minutes, go back to work. At lunch time, we'll play, go for a walk, and take a longer break.

Bashir spends more time with me each day than any of my other friends. He's a fun companion; he makes me laugh and I enjoy his company. He's also good security; if I'm engrossed at the computer he lets me know when someone is near the house or at the front door.

However, he wasn't born this way; as a puppy he was rowdy, he got into trouble occasionally, and he thought he should be the center of attention all the time. It took time, training, and good parenting to teach Bashir the rules I wanted him to observe. But it was all worth it because today he is a wonderful canine best friend!

The Least You Need to Know

- In a natural situation, a puppy would never leave his mom at 8 to 10 weeks of age.

- We need to be our Yorkie's adoptive parent by acting as a parent as we teach him.

- A good leader is a good parent and teaches the puppy good social manners.

- Later, when your Yorkie is mentally mature, he can become your best friend.

Chapter 5

Understanding Canine Communication and Learning

In This Chapter

- Tuning in to canine communication
- Learning that body postures are language
- Listening to the sounds
- Helping your dog learn

Dogs communicate very well. If you have doubts, think about how many times your dog has wanted you to do something and actually gained your cooperation so you did it! You know when he wants a cookie or he has a desire to play. You know, too, when he has to go outside. And should you go somewhere in the car and he wants to go with you, well, you know that, too!

Dogs are so good at communicating (and at training people) that we often don't think about how they are conveying their wants or needs to us; we just know. We have learned from them. However, if you take a more conscious look at your dog, and watch and listen, then you can make that communication that much better.

Communication works two ways. When you understand your dog better, you can also more effectively convey your ideas, wants, desires, and requirements to him. How much easier life is with communication!

Canine Communication

For people, communication is the process of exchanging thoughts, ideas, needs, desires, goals, feelings, and much more. We convey these ideas by talking about them (to someone or via a recording), writing them down (handwritten or via computer), or singing (personally or recorded).

We also communicate through body language, and although we don't often consciously think about it, it is important. When body language isn't visible (such as when sending e-mails) miscommunication is more common.

Dogs tend to think about things they want or things they want to do. Dogs want to go for a walk, want to play, want food, want to snuggle, or need to go outside. They communicate primarily through body postures, facial expressions, and tail movements. These are all part of what is called body language. They also use verbalizations about as much as they do body language.

Dog Talk

Communication for people is the exchange of thoughts or ideas using speech, writing, or body language. Subtracting writing, it is the same for dogs.

Brenda Aloff, an expert at canine communication and the author of the book, *Canine Body Language* (Dogwise, 2005) says, "Living with dogs means that you must work at finding a common language between the two of you.

This is frustrating in the extreme for both species. While humans are constantly trying to talk to dogs as if they were people, dogs are constantly trying to talk to humans as if they were dogs. This causes endless misunderstandings."

When you understand your dog better, you can eliminate many misunderstandings and frustrations for both of you. In addition, training your dog, whether for household rules or obedience training, will be much easier.

Watching His Body Movements

Your dog has very complex body language. The movements, postures, and positions of his head, ears, eyes, mouth, tongue, tail, and entire body can convey a variety of meanings. For example, a dog standing tall yet relaxed, with upright ears, open mouth, relaxed tongue, and wagging tail, exudes confidence without aggression. Each body part, alone or with others, demonstrates what the dog is feeling.

Those feelings and postures can be enhanced by colorings or markings, especially on the face and tail. For example, when the eyes are outlined in black, with tan spots above the eyes, any movement of the eyes is exaggerated. This can make communicating with other dogs easier.

Dogs lacking some of these markings, such as an all-white or all-black dog, are somewhat at a disadvantage and could potentially be misunderstood. A tail-less dog, whether naturally tail-less or docked, similar to Yorkies, loses all the communication that a long tail provides. Misunderstandings in the dog's world could be minor, primarily because dogs use more than one body part to convey emotions, but occasionally a dog fight can ensue.

Bet You Didn't Know

Dogs can put cause and effect together. Your dog may have once tried to get your attention by tilting his head to the side while whining quietly. If you responded in the manner he wanted, he will remember that. That's deliberate communication.

Some Emotional Body Postures

When you understand what your dog is trying to convey to you through his body language, you can communicate better with him yourself. You can tailor your training techniques when you see that he's worried or frustrated; you can give him more confidence when you see that he's insecure or afraid; and you can applaud his efforts when he's accomplished something and is proud of himself.

- If your Yorkie is fearful, he will lower his body almost to the ground, with elbows and hocks bent. His tail will be down and close to his hips, and his head and ears will be down. He may lick his nose.

- Very fearful Yorkies—those so afraid that they may bite if cornered or pushed too hard—will also have a lowered body posture. The head and ears will be lowered, and the back of the lips will be pulled back, making the dog almost look like he's smiling. The eyes may look forward at the potential threat and then glance away. The tail will be tucked up against the hips, and will be still.

- A submissive but not necessarily fearful Yorkie may roll over and bare his belly. The tail may be tucked and still (if worried) or tucked and wagging (if simply submissive). The eyes will look away.

- A dominant Yorkie—one with the potential to take his dominance too far (with the possibility of a bite or fight)—will have all his body language moving forward. He will be on the tips of his toes leaning forward, with his head forward and his eyes staring hard at the object of his interest. The ears will be lifted and facing forward, and the tail will be up and wagging slowly or stiffly, or still. His hackles will probably be up.

- A confidant Yorkie who is interested or alert, but who has no need or desire to bite or fight, will stand tall but also be relaxed. He will not be leaning forward. His head will be high but relaxed, with ears up and forward, and his hackles will be down. His tail will be wagging.

An eager, happy Yorkie will not be standing still; he will dance, circle, or bounce up and down. His eyes will be toward you; his ears will be up and down, with openings toward you; and his tail will be wagging happily. He may lower his front end to bow, an invitation to play.

Dogs communicate with each other very effectively through body language, eye contact, and verbalizations.

This is just a brief example of some postures. Every breed and every individual dog has its own characteristics. For example, terriers (as with Yorkies) stare. This technique is used by terriers to signal a hunt (a mouse has been spotted or there is movement in the grass), but Yorkies also learn to use it on their owners. Staring is usually an attention-getting device, because, when stared at, most owners respond, "What do you want?" and the dog could end up going for a walk or playing ball.

Bet You Didn't Know

Even though many dogs, especially terriers, always seem ready for a scuffle or scrap, most dogs do not want to fight. In a fight, dogs get hurt. Calming signals in canine body language defuse tense situations.

Commonly Seen Signals

As you train your dog, you will learn to recognize other signals that are part of most dogs' body language. For example, if your training is getting too serious, your dog may yawn at you. He's not sleepy! This is called a calming signal; your dog is basically saying, "Relax!" Some dogs, when they are getting frustrated or bored, will look away from you. This is the time to take a training break for a few minutes and rethink your training technique so that you can approach it from another angle. Watch your dog, get to know him, and use his means of communication to your advantage:

- If he looks away, he may feel pressured or you may be staring harshly at him. Or depending on his personality, he may be avoiding your commands.

- He may also turn away from you if you're angry or frustrated and he feels it.

- If your dog freezes in place, he may be afraid to do something. He may be worried or afraid to try something new.

- If your dog refuses to do what you ask in place; you may be coming on too strong in your training approach.

Listening to Canine Verbalizations

When your dog is communicating with other dogs, the sounds your dog makes are not as important as his body language, but that doesn't mean they aren't important. Just this morning, one of my dogs was outside and began barking at a delivery man next door. The two dogs in the house couldn't see the dog outside, but they could hear him and knew that his alarm bark meant something was going on. They immediately ran to the door, barking their own alarm barks.

I think the easiest way to understand the relationship between body language and verbalizations is this:

🦴 Verbalizations back up body language. Your dog conveys a message with his movements, gestures, and signals, and his sounds reinforce those movements.

🦴 Verbalizations can attract more attention. When he is heard, then people (and other dogs) look at him and can see his body language.

🦴 People tend to consciously pay more attention to sounds.

Tone Is More Important

All dogs, no matter where they're from, speak the same canine language. Although some breeds, such as Basenjis, are more prone to breed-specific sounds such as yowls; and hounds are more prone to bay; all dogs can understand each other.

A huge part of that is because the tone of voice is more important than the actual "words" or sounds. For example, every dog who wants to play will use higher than normal vocalizations. Every dog who is scared or hurt will use high-pitched howls or yips. And angry dogs use deeper-than-normal sounds or growls.

When dog owners understand this, it makes communicating with our dogs much easier. And it explains, too, why so many women have trouble assuming a parental leadership role with their dogs. Most women have a higher-pitched voice that lacks authority to the dog. However, if women consciously bring their voice down, they can convey authority.

Bet You Didn't Know

When Molly, a Standard Poodle, gets up in the morning, she greets her owner with a lovely front leg stretch—the hips high and the front legs stretched out in front. This is a relaxed, comfortable bow that conveys affection and security.

Training (and living with) your Yorkie will be much easier when you can communicate with him.

Dogs Teach Themselves, Too

My youngest dog is 15 months and has recently discovered that he can use his voice for more than just reactive alarm barking. He has been experimenting with small barks, whines, and other sounds. I see him making a sound and then paying attention to the reaction he gets, and it's been fascinating.

When he made a loud, annoying, full-voiced whine as I worked at the computer, I used a deep growly voice to tell him, "Knock it off!" My voice mimicked a mother dog telling her puppy that he made a mistake and immediately my puppy stopped the whine. And I haven't heard him use it since.

However, when I was playing with him and he made some soft, playful barks, I answered back in a happy tone of voice, "Do you want to play? Huh?" He has since used that tone of voice again during play sessions.

By paying attention to the reactions he gets, he's learning what sounds work for him in a positive manner and which do not. It will be fun to see where he goes with this. He's smart enough to learn from his experiences.

Bet You Didn't Know

Scratching can be a signal that portrays stress. During training or in social situations, a dog may scratch his collar with a back leg. He doesn't have an itch; he's just saying he's uncomfortable with the situation.

Helping Your Dog Learn

You may be using some of your dog's body language and verbalizations without knowing it because some are very similar to our own. A person who is confidant yet not aggressive or pushy stands tall yet relaxed and uses a calm tone of voice. A bully or pushy person who is trying to get his way stands tall and leans into people, invading personal space, and tends to be loud. A worrier pulls into himself, looks away without making eye contact, and uses small hand gestures and a quiet, shaky voice.

You can communicate more easily with your dog if you can copy some of your dog's body language and verbalizations. But pay attention to the reactions you get from your dog. After all, you can both learn from each other and adapt. If something doesn't work; try something else. And don't be afraid to laugh:

> If your dog is having a hard time with a new lesson, take some pressure off him. Instead of facing your dog straight on, turn so that you are at an angle, facing toward him and to the front. Make sure that your body language is relaxed, look at your dog (his paws, body, tail, face) without staring into his eyes, and smile without showing teeth. This conveys to him, "Hey, it's okay. No pressure!" Use a calm yet happy tone of voice.

> If your dog is getting into trouble, especially when he understands that he's doing something you don't want him to do, stand tall, look him in the eye, and don't flinch. You have just conveyed your position as the dominant family member. Use a deep, growly tone of voice.

🦴 At the end of a training session, lift your hands high over your head, and then, with a big smile on your face, bring both hands down to your knees as you bend your body at the waist. You can also hop at the same time. You have just invited your dog to play! Use a higher pitched than normal, happy tone of voice.

The Least You Need to Know

🦴 Misunderstandings, hard feelings, frustrations, and anger happen when a dog and owner don't understand each other and are failing to communicate.

🦴 Your dog has a complex, rich system of body language that can convey a lot about how he's feeling.

🦴 Although verbalizations aren't as important to your dog's communication, they are important and you can use them to convey your messages to your Yorkie.

🦴 Pay attention to your dog's communications with you and his reactions to you trying to communicate with him. You can teach each other.

Chapter 6

Establishing Household Rules

In This Chapter

- ☙ Using your parenting skills
- ☙ Learning the importance of rules
- ☙ Deciding on household rules
- ☙ Teaching your Yorkie

If your Yorkie was able to decide on his own household rules, he would probably stake out the most comfortable sofa as his own. He would eat there, drag all his toys up there, and would growl should anyone else approach his sofa. His favorite chew toys might include your shoes and socks or the pillow off your bed. He would chase the family cat whenever he wanted and the refrigerator would open automatically whenever he approached it.

Although that might be the ideal life for a Yorkie (and hopefully your Yorkie hasn't already started doing too many of those behaviors) it is not the ideal life for you. After all, this is your house. You pay the rent or mortgage; you buy the dog food and pay the vet bills; and you have every right to establish household rules. Those rules, combined with basic obedience training, should help control your Yorkie's behavior in the house and yard, and protect your belongings.

> **Yorkie Smarts**
>
> One of the most common mistakes Yorkie owners make is that they spoil their Yorkie instead of lead him. Your Yorkie is tiny, but he's still a dog, and dogs need leaders.

Deciding what rules you want to establish in the house will take some thought. Talk to your family and figure out what's important to all of you. Then, everyone must consistently enforce those rules. If your Yorkie has already found out that some of these behaviors are fun, don't despair; we can change his mind.

Use Your Parenting Skills

In Chapter 4, we discussed your parenting skills and why they are important. If you are not yet comfortable acting as your Yorkie's parent, go back to Chapter 4 and re-read it. Implement as many of those skills as you can, especially those pertaining to being a good leader.

Keep in mind, your Yorkie's mother was his first teacher and leader. If he bit her too roughly, she would growl at him until he stopped. If he was too rough with his littermates, she would correct him. When he was good, she would lick him with affection. She showed him what it was like to be a dog. She was also his first leader.

> **Yorkie Smarts**
>
> The best **leader** for a Yorkie is fair, firm, and demands respect. To be a good leader, think of yourself as your Yorkie's parent.

As with all youngsters, your Yorkie puppy needs leadership. The *leader* teaches him what the rules are and how to behave. Without leadership, he would have to make up his own rules and would be insecure and fearful or bossy and aggressive; depending on his personality. Although you may have gotten a dog because you wanted a canine best friend, right now your Yorkie needs a leader. Later, when he's all grown up, well trained, and mentally mature, he can be your best friend.

Your Yorkie Needs Rules

Household rules give your Yorkie some guidelines as to what is and isn't socially acceptable behavior. These rules are not designed to make your Yorkie's life difficult (or yours) but instead they are to help you, your family, and your dog live together peacefully. After all, you and your family wouldn't like living in a dog kennel; so let's keep your house nice and comfortable, yet teach your dog to live with you.

When you establish these rules very early—as soon as your Yorkie puppy joins your family—he never learns the wrong behavior. For example, do you want him underfoot in the kitchen? Tiny dogs are hard to see when you've got your hands full. Start teaching the puppy now, as a young puppy, exactly what you expect of him. He's capable of learning; you just need to teach him.

If you have adopted an older puppy or an adult, or if your Yorkie already has some established bad habits, you are going to have to work a little harder to teach him the new rules. But don't give up, you can do it; your dog can learn, and the two of you can live peacefully together.

Yorkie Smarts

By 8 to 10 weeks of age, your Yorkie's brain is fully functional and capable of incredible learning. Although he is a baby physically, he is ready and willing to learn.

Watch Out!

Don't allow your Yorkie to beg for food; this is a very bad habit that can easily escalate into snapping or food stealing.

Deciding the Rules

When trying to decide what rules you would like to establish, keep in mind what your dog will grow up to be. A toy breed dog is much easier to deal with on the furniture than a giant breed dog with a heavy coat, so you may decide to allow your Yorkie on the furniture. I like to cuddle with my dogs, so they are invited on the furniture. My mother, on the other hand, likes to keep her furniture free of dog hair, so her dogs are not allowed on her furniture.

Your rules should take into account your personal likes and dislikes, your daily routine, and any other desires. Perhaps a half-chewed dog bone hidden under a sofa cushion would make you very unhappy; if so, keep the dog off the furniture.

One of the most important household rules is that of housetraining. Your Yorkie should never relieve himself inside your house unless he does so in a doggy litter box. Relieving himself anywhere he wants in the house is disgusting, dirty, rude, and disrespectful to you. Chapter 7 discusses housetraining in greater detail; I felt it was important enough to warrant its own chapter. For right now just understand that it is a very important household rule.

Another important rule is that of biting people. Your Yorkie should never use his teeth on you or anyone else; even as a puppy. Again, it is very disrespectful, and even though he's tiny, it's still dangerous. Even tiny dogs can be taken from you and put into quarantine should they bite someone. And after quarantine, depending on the situation and the laws in your city, county, or state, the dog can be put to sleep. In addition, you could be sued for damages, emotional distress, and more. Just as with housetraining, I feel biting is also important enough to deserve a chapter of its own; we'll talk about biting in greater detail in Chapter 8.

The following list has a few other suggestions for some household rules:

- We mentioned the dangers of having a tiny Yorkie in the kitchen, but let's look at this again. Although Yorkies can be very quick about staying out from underfoot, they are also easy to step on. If you have a hot pan on the stove or a platter with dinner on it, you don't want to trip over a tiny dog, risking harm to the dog and yourself. Never mind the potential of ruining dinner!

- Is your Yorkie allowed to beg for food while you're eating? This isn't an acceptable habit, either. The puppy who begs for food usually ends up being a big pest, pawing legs, licking hands, or even stealing food. If you don't want to allow begging, make sure no one feeds the puppy as they eat.

- We have also already mentioned the idea of allowing your Yorkie up on the furniture. This is a purely personal decision. After you make up your mind, however, you can't change a few months down the road or if you get a new sofa.

- Many dog owners like to have their dog sleep with them. Unfortunately, this is a bad habit and an especially bad one for Yorkies. Your Yorkie needs his own bed (his crate), and it can be (and should be) in your bedroom. But he should not sleep in your bed, for two reasons. First of all, it is too dangerous for him. A tiny dog can easily get trapped and squashed should an adult person roll over on him in the middle of the night. In addition, if the Yorkie sleeps with you, he will think he's your equal—after all, he sleeps in the leader's bed!

> **Watch Out!**
>
> If your Yorkie is already sleeping on the bed and growls at you when you move or ask him to get off the bed, call a dog trainer or behaviorist for help right away. This can be a serious behavior problem that has been known to end up with the dog biting the owner.

- Do you want to restrict certain parts of the house? If you wish to keep the puppy out of the kids' rooms so that he won't get into their stuff, that's fine. If you have a nice formal living room, teach him to stay in the family room and restrict him from the living room. In fact, as I've mentioned before, the puppy *does not* and *should not* have free run of the house. To restrict his access, close doors and use baby gates to keep him in the rooms where he is allowed.

🦴 Teach him to wait at all doorways so he doesn't dash out each time a door is opened. Not only can this keep him from being stepped on, it can also keep him out of areas where you don't want him—such as those restricted rooms. In addition, this habit can also be applied to doors to the outside as well as gates. Teaching him this can help keep him safe, too.

Some household rules, such as teaching your Yorkie not to dash out open doors, are very important.

🦴 Teach him to relax. In Chapter 12, I talk with a dog trainer, Martin Deeley, who emphasizes the importance of teaching dogs that they can lie down and relax; they do not need to entertain us all the time or be the center of attention constantly. Your Yorkie needs to learn he can lie down and relax.

What else is important to you? Think about it. What will make life with a dog easier?

Teaching Your Yorkie

Teaching your Yorkie is not difficult when you get the hang of it. As much as possible, prevent problem behaviors from happening. For example, if you know your Yorkie likes to raid the bathroom trashcan, put it away. However, when you're in the bathroom, set the trashcan out in the middle of the floor. When your Yorkie sniffs the can, tell him, "No! Leave it alone!" using that firm, no-nonsense voice we talked about in Chapter 5. When he then ignores the trashcan, praise him, "Good choice! Yeah!" However, when you go to leave the room again, put the trashcan away. One training session will not teach him, but repeated training sessions will.

Now, let's diagram what you're doing:

- When you are not watching the dog, or are unavailable for teaching, prevent the problem from happening. That means the dog is in his crate or the problem is put away.

- When you can teach the dog, make the problem accessible.

- Have a collar on the dog so he can't run away from you.

- When he doesn't obey, stop him with leash and voice.

- Then show him what to do instead and praise and reward him for doing it.

- When he does the right thing on his own, really enthusiastically praise him!

- Again, when you are not watching the dog, or are unavailable for training, prevent the problem from happening. That means the dog is in his crate or the problem is put away.

You need to teach your puppy what is acceptable and what is not. When he grabs the sofa cushion, take it away from him and hand him one of his toys instead. When he picks up your good leather shoes, take them away, put them in the closet, close the closet door, and hand the puppy one of his toys.

Yorkie Smarts

When your Yorkie is doing something right, give him permission to do it and praise him. For example, if he picks up his toy instead of your shoe, tell him, "Get your toy! Good boy!" Reinforce that good behavior!

Some household rules depend on your preferences: do you want your Yorkie on the furniture or not?

Family Unity

When you establish the household rules, make sure everyone in the household will accept them and enforce them. If your daughter sneaks the Yorkie food from her plate, the dog will continue to beg from the table. If you correct him but your daughter feeds him, he will be confused and his behavior erratic. Everyone must be consistent with the rules.

Posting a list of the rules in a prominent location works for many puppy owners. List a command, such as "No Begging!" so that everyone is using the same language, and a list of the rules themselves. Put it up on the refrigerator where everyone will see it on a daily basis.

Patience and Consistency

Training takes time; you need to teach these new rules over and over again. After all, your dog has no idea why you don't want him to dash out the front gate. As far as he's concerned, things are happening in the front yard that he should be a part of. He has no concept that being in the street may mean that he could be hit by a car.

However, if you praise his cooperation, even when you've given him no choice, he will learn that it's worth his while to cooperate. "Ah ha! When I sit at the gate and don't dash out, I get petting and a treat. Hmmm ... I can do that!"

You also need to prevent problem behaviors from happening because a lot of these are fun. Raiding the kitchen trashcan and finding tidbits in there is fun; that turns it into a self-rewarding behavior, and you already know that self-rewarding behaviors will continue to happen until you stop them.

In addition, keep in mind that changing habits takes time. If you have ever tried to change a bad habit—smoking or overeating, for example—you know that it takes time to break the bad habit and time to rebuild a good replacement habit. The same applies to your dog. So be patient and help him learn good household habits.

Last but certainly not least, Yorkies are not mentally mature until at least two years of age. So your 6-, 12-, or even 18-month-old Yorkie is not mentally grown up. Puppies don't always think before they do things; teach him what to do, but don't rely on his good behavior yet.

The Least You Need to Know

- Your parenting and leadership skills are needed to teach your dog what you want him to do.

- Household rules teach your Yorkie what is socially acceptable in your home.

- Establish rules that will work for your family and household, and then make sure everyone enforces them consistently.

- Be patient and consistent as you train your Yorkie.

Chapter 7

Housetraining Is Vital

In This Chapter

- 🦴 Housetraining tiny dogs
- 🦴 Training with the litter box
- 🦴 Putting the crate to good use
- 🦴 Having no excuses!

As a behavioral consultant and dog trainer, I get far too many calls from the owners of toy breed dogs, including Yorkshire Terriers, complaining about their dogs' housetraining skills. The dogs are usually poorly trained, have multiple accidents per week (and sometimes per day), and the owners are frustrated.

Housetraining is one of the most important social manners your Yorkie needs to learn. This process involves teaching him where he should (and should not) relieve himself as well as learning to try and relieve himself when you ask him to.

Housetraining Toy Breed Dogs

A dog who knows where to relieve himself, where not to relieve himself, and how to try to relieve himself on command is a welcome companion. A dog who doesn't have these skills is not only unwelcome in other people's homes and in public places, but he's damaging his owner's home, including the carpet.

As a dog trainer, my students frequently ask me housetraining questions. How can I teach my puppy to go outside? What should I do when my dog has an accident in the house? Why does he have to go outside so often? To many dog owners, housetraining seems to be mystical and incredibly difficult. But it doesn't have to be that way. When I housetrain a new puppy of my own, I go outside with the puppy so I can teach her, I make up a schedule for trips outside, I restrict the puppy's freedom in the house, and I use a kennel crate. With these tools, my dogs learn housetraining rules with little difficulty, and yours should, too.

Dog Talk

Housetraining refers to the process of teaching the dog where to relieve himself and where not to relieve himself.

I am often amazed at the number of Yorkies who are not well housetrained. I have even heard breeders say that it is very difficult or even impossible to housetrain Yorkies (or other toy breed dogs). It may very well be impossible if the breeder or owner doesn't take the time to train the dog correctly. It may also be impossible if the breeder or owner makes too many excuses. However, there is absolutely no reason to live with a dog who isn't housetrained!

I don't know where the myth got started that toy breed dogs are impossible to housetrain, but I have heard it said about several breeds, including Yorkies and Papillons. Perhaps because toy breed dogs are so small, an accident is easy to overlook. Or perhaps it's because a toy breed dog has to take more steps than bigger dogs to get to the door. I don't know where the myth came from but I wish it would disappear!

When housetraining your Yorkie, you are teaching him where to relieve himself as well as not to relieve himself in the house.

Toy dogs are just as capable of being well housetrained as any other breed of dog of any size. They do sometimes take a little while longer to develop bladder control (they are tiny and that bladder doesn't hold much!) but with your help, training, consistency, and patience they are capable of doing it.

Litter Boxes for Dogs

Litter boxes for tiny dogs have been in use for many years. Most dog owners use large cat litter boxes, complete with either cat litter, sod (grass growing in dirt), dirt or sand, or one of the new commercial litters made expressly for dog litter boxes. There are pros and cons to each of these:

- Cat litter can work as long as you choose one that does not form clumps when liquid hits it. These litters, which contain a type of clay, can cause major internal problems should the dog ingest some of the litter. But cat litter made from recycled paper, wheat, or other natural products will work fine.

✍ Some dog owners choose to provide a piece of sod for their dog inside, getting a new piece of sod at a garden store every weekend. This can work if the sod is in a waterproof box such as a litter box or a mortar pan (which is similar to a large litter box). If the sod is in the house much longer than a week, the urine odor will become quite strong and the sod will die.

✍ Dirt and sand are messy, easily tracked throughout the house, and won't provide any odor control at all. They are easy to replace, however, and inexpensive.

✍ The new commercial litters made for dog litter boxes are more expensive than dirt, sand, or sod, but are excellent for odor control.

✍ The absorbent pads made for housetraining puppies can also be used for litter box training. If you use these, place the pads in a litter box rather than straight on the floor. After all, you want to teach the dog to relieve himself in this box on the pads rather than anywhere on the floor.

Do not use newspaper to housetrain your dog to relieve himself in the house. This will teach your dog that he can relieve himself any time a newspaper is on the floor, and that might include your Sunday paper!

Watch Out!

Beware of the housetraining litter box setups that use fake grass or carpet to teach your dog to relieve himself in the house. These have taught far too many dogs that relieving themselves on any carpet is fine!

Deciding on a Litter Box

Litter box training is definitely not for all dogs and all dog owners. Some dogs can be very resistant to this training and can develop some bad housetraining habits. It is also much more successful with very small dogs, such as tiny Yorkies, and less successful for larger dogs who produce, obviously, more urine and feces and hence, smell.

Litter boxes for small dogs can work if …

- The training begins when the dog is a young puppy.

- The owner works long hours and the dog must remain in the house all day with no one to take him outside.

- The owner is an invalid or is housebound.

- The dog and owner live in a climate where the weather outside would be dangerous for a tiny dog.

However, if the dog and owner are able to get outside on a regular basis, I prefer teaching the dog to relieve himself outside. It's easier, usually more dependable, and definitely more natural to the dog.

Yorkie Smarts

Dog litter boxes must be cleaned daily at a minimum. However, some dogs will not go back to the box after the box has been used. This means to housetrain the dog reliably, you must provide two boxes for the dog or must clean up after the dog several times each day.

Training the Dog to Use a Box

Housetraining a dog to use the box follows the same rules you would use to take a dog outside. The only difference is that you will take your dog to his box instead of outside. As you continue to read this chapter, as we discuss housetraining in greater detail, follow these instructions, but take your dog, on leash, to his box rather than outside. There will also be notes in the text concerning litter box training when it varies from the other housetraining instructions.

Crate Training Your Yorkie

A crate (often called a kennel or a kennel crate) is a travel carrier for dogs. Originally used for dogs being transported on airplanes, they are now used to help dogs learn housetraining skills. A crate works by taking advantage of the puppy's own instincts to keep his bed clean. Very few puppies or dogs will soil their bed, so they learn (with your help) not to go in their bed and to go where you wish them to go.

Three Types of Crates

There are three types of crates available and each has its own good points and bad points. You need to look at your needs and the needs of your dog and choose which crate would work best.

Watch Out!

Puppies bought from a pet store often have trouble learning crate training because they have spent too much time in a cage. Because they must relieve themselves in the cage, they lose their inhibition about soiling their bed.

The first type of crate (and the most popular) is made of plastic or fiberglass. It has a metal barred door and barred windows for ventilation on each side. These come in two parts, top and bottom, and are easily cleaned. They are relatively lightweight and although somewhat bulky, are easily stored. Because they have solid sides, these crates provide the puppy with a feeling of security; much as a den.

Heavy gauge wire crates are more like a cage. The open sides provide good air circulation and in hot weather, this is wonderful. Because they are open, though, some dogs—especially many tiny Yorkies—feel exposed and vulnerable. These crates are heavy, although most brands do fold up flat. They usually have a metal tray in the bottom that can be pulled out to be cleaned.

The third type is often called a carry bag rather than a crate, but it's essentially a soft-sided crate for carrying toy breed dogs, cats, ferrets, and other small pets. These can be very useful for transporting your Yorkie to the vet's office or groomer, but these

Yorkie Smarts

You may wish to have a plastic crate for use at home and a soft-sided carrying bag for errands around town.

should not be used for daily training. With the soft sides, these carry bags collapse too easily, can be chewed through, and don't provide enough security for you or your puppy. Keep in mind that if you want to use these for traveling, the soft-sided carriers provide no protection to your Yorkie if you are in an accident.

Crate Size

Choose a crate that will allow your puppy to stand up, turn around, and stretch out. Too much room is not better. If the crate is too big, the puppy can relieve himself in a back corner and still have room to get away from it. The purpose of using a crate to housetrain your puppy is to utilize his instinct to keep his bed clean. A cat crate will probably fit your tiny Yorkie just fine!

Your Yorkie's Personal Space

As your Yorkie is introduced to the crate, it will become his own personal space. It's his den or cave—a place where he can hide his favorite toys or bones. He can retreat to his crate when he's tired or doesn't feel good. He will sleep in his crate at night and will spend some time there during the day when you're unable to supervise him.

Don't let the family cat camp out in your Yorkie's crate and make sure the kids don't store their dolls or toys there, either. This is your Yorkie's personal space.

Crate training your Yorkie is a very important part of the house-training process.

Keep It Positive!

The crate should never be used for punishment. Never put your Yorkie in his crate as you are scolding him. Never yell at him or berate him while he's in the crate; not only will these episodes make him think the crate is a bad place, but those types of corrections are not good dog-training techniques.

Introducing the Crate

You want your Yorkie to think the crate is a fun place all his own, so how you introduce him to it is important. Place the crate in the living room and fasten the door open so it can't close unexpectedly and startle him.

Watch Out!

Take care not to rush the introduction of the crate, as this could panic your dog. Make this as positive as possible.

Have a few dog treats, and toss them one at a time toward the crate. Let him grab and eat those treats. A little while later, toss a treat or two into the crate and let him get those. Later still or even the next day, let him chase a couple of treats into the crate.

When he goes in and out with no trouble, start feeding him in the crate, but continue to keep the door open. When he eats in the crate with no fuss, close the door behind him. Do *not* let him out if he throws a fit! Open the door only when he is calm and quiet. If he cries, barks, and scratches at the door, ignore him.

Using the Crate

Put the crate in your bedroom at night so your Yorkie can hear you, smell you, and be close to you all night. This is eight hours of closeness that you probably couldn't find the time for at any other time of day. Yorkies need time with their owner, and although these nighttime hours don't require you to do anything except sleep, to your dog they are wonderful.

In addition, with the puppy close to you, you can hear him if he gets restless and needs to go outside. If he doesn't have to go outside and is just moving around, you can reach over, tap the top of the crate, and tell him, "No! Quiet!" However, if your puppy's restlessness continues, take him outside.

During the day, you can move the crate around. Put it in the living room if the family is gathered there, or have it near the laundry room if you're folding clothes.

Then put the puppy in his crate for a few minutes here and there; whenever you are too busy to supervise him. Because he has to spend many hours in his crate at night, try to limit his time in it during the day to short periods. Having 20 minutes here and 30 minutes there is okay as long as he gets plenty of attention, exercise, and time with you in between times in the crate.

Bet You Didn't Know

An exercise pen is a playpen for dogs. Foldable, portable, small fence sections can be set up in the house to give your Yorkie more freedom than his crate allows yet at the same time restrict his freedom in the house, thereby limiting potential mistakes. His litter box can be placed in here so he can relieve himself should he be left alone for hours at a time.

Don't Abuse the Crate

Other than at night, don't leave your Yorkie in the crate for more than two to three hours at a time. During the day, he needs time to stretch his legs, run, and play.

If you and other family members are away from the house all day, make some arrangements for your dog. Perhaps he can go to a doggy daycare or you can ask a neighbor to take him out and walk him. Many teenage kids will walk dogs for a few dollars a week. If you can't make other arrangements, then a secure, safe, covered dog run or an exercise pen with a litter box might be the best answer.

Prevention Better Than Correction

A crate can help you prevent problems from happening. If you can prevent the puppy from learning bad habits, training will be much easier. In addition, your puppy won't be able to cause as much damage, which reduces your—and your puppy's—stress!

When you can't supervise your Yorkie puppy, put him outside in a safe place in the yard or put him in his crate. By ensuring he doesn't get into trouble, you're preventing problem behavior. He will never learn that it's fun to chew up the sofa cushions if he never gets a chance to do it! By preventing the bad behavior, you can also ensure the dog learns good habits. The puppy learns to chew on the toys you give him rather than learning to be destructive.

The Housetraining Process

With all the conflicting advice and misinformation about housetraining that bombards new puppy owners, it's amazing that so many dogs do eventually become well housetrained. However, housetraining doesn't have to be mysterious or confusing. If you understand your puppy's need to keep his bed clean, limit your puppy's freedom, teach him what you want and where you want it, and set a good schedule, your puppy will cooperate.

Take Him Outside or to His Box

With your Yorkie on leash so he can't dash away from you, ignore you, or go play, take your Yorkie outside (or to his litter box) where you want him to relieve himself. Stand with him, but don't interact with him. When the puppy starts to sniff and circle, just watch. After he has started to relieve himself, tell him softly, "Go potty! Good boy to go potty!" (Using, of course, whatever vocabulary you wish to use.) When he has completed his business, praise him even more.

You'll need to take him to this particular spot every time he needs to go for several weeks. Yes, weeks! You cannot simply send the puppy outside or send him in the direction of his box. If you do, how do you know he has done what he needs to do? How can you teach him the command if you aren't there? And how can you praise him for doing what needs to be done if, again, you aren't there? Even worse, if you let him have free run of the house when he hasn't relieved himself, it's then your fault if he comes in and has an accident.

Many dog owners come to my training classes complaining about their dog's lack of housetraining skills and, invariably, they say, "I send my dog outside, but when he comes back in, he goes on the floor!" In these situations, the dog is going outside alone. The owner lets the dog in a few minutes later but has no idea whether the dog has actually relieved himself outside. (Even if he has, the owner wasn't there to praise the dog for going in the right place or to teach him the proper command.) When the dog is allowed back in the house and relieves himself on the floor, he is yelled at. Granted getting yelled at is negative attention, but it is still attention. In these cases, I tell the owners they have housetrained their dog all right; they have trained him to go in the house!

Yorkie Smarts

If your Yorkie is young but hasn't had an accident in a while, don't assume he's housetrained. Instead, simply realize you are doing everything correctly and pat yourself on the back!

Housetraining is a very important skill, and many dogs (including many Yorkies) end up at animal control shelters all over the country because they haven't been well housetrained. Take your time while your Yorkie is young and teach this correctly; it's too important to take lightly.

Teaching a Command

It's important that your Yorkie puppy understand his command ("Go potty," "Get busy," or whatever phrase you wish to use) to relieve himself. If you take the puppy (or later, the dog) to visit someone, it's very nice to be able to tell the dog to relieve himself before going inside the house. The same thing works when you're traveling. If you stop to get gas, you can then tell the dog to try and relieve himself, and even if his bladder isn't full, he can try.

Start using a command when you first start housetraining the puppy. Tell him "Go potty!" (using the vocabulary that is comfortable to you) and praising him when he does relieve himself. "Good boy to go potty!"

As his housetraining gets better and more reliable, use the commands when you're out on walks so he learns to go potty in different places. Some puppies learn that they are to relieve themselves only in their backyard or in their litter box, and their owners have a difficult time teaching them that it's okay to do it elsewhere. So teach the puppy that when you give him this command, he is to try, even if he can only squeeze out a drop!

Creatures of Habit

Dogs, as with many people, are creatures of habit. Housetraining is much easier if the young Yorkie eats, sleeps, and goes outside on a fairly regular schedule. Variations are allowed, of course, but not too many.

Keep in mind that a very young puppy will need to eat two to three times per day. He'll need to go outside to relieve himself after each meal. He'll also need to go outside after playing, when waking up from a nap, and about every two hours in between. After a nap or after sleeping at night, carry your puppy outside, as he may need to relieve himself right away.

As your Yorkie grows up, he may eat only two meals a day but will still have to go outside after each meal. He'll also need to relieve himself after playtimes, after naps, and first thing in the morning.

Take all these things into account when you set up a schedule. Take into consideration, too, your normal routine. You may have to make some adjustments in your routine to get the puppy outside often enough, but that goes hand in hand with having a puppy!

As your Yorkie puppy gets older and develops more bladder and bowel control, he'll be able to go longer between trips outside, but this is a gradual process. Many puppies can be considered house-trained and reliable by five to six months of age as long as they aren't required to hold it too long. However, it is not unusual for some puppies to need a strict schedule and many trips outside until six, seven, and even eight months of age. Just as some children potty-train at different ages and rates, so do puppies. A puppy is house-trained and reliable when he is ready and able to do it.

Gotta Go—Now!

When you've set up a schedule for your Yorkie puppy, you need to follow it. In addition, you want to teach him to notify you when he needs to go out.

When I have a puppy at home as my husband and I do right now, I use my voice a lot as a training tool. As I walk the puppy toward the back door, I ask him, "Sweetie pie, do you have to go potty?" in a higher-pitched than normal, happy tone of voice. As the puppy reacts to my tone of voice and as he learns the words, he will get excited and dash toward the door. Eventually, when he needs to go he will come looking for me, will make eye contact, and then will dash to the door.

When Archer, our puppy, figured this out, I praised him, gave him a treat, and ran to the backyard with him, telling him what a special puppy he was! Although this might seem to be somewhat silly, it isn't. A key part of housetraining is teaching the puppy how to let you know he needs to go. When Archer came to me, got my attention, made eye contact (so he knew I was paying attention to him), and then dashed to the door; well, then I knew he understood the process—and that's a huge leap in learning!

> **Watch Out!**
>
> I don't teach my dogs to bark when they want to go outside because, as a dog trainer, I hear many complaints about barking dogs. Teaching a dog to bark to go outside can be emphasizing a potential behavior problem.

As the dog gains more control and can go longer between trips outside, I will check with him once in a while, "Do you have to go potty?" If he does, he will dance and wiggle and head toward the door. I will, of course, praise him and let him out. If he just stares at me but doesn't move toward the door, that means he doesn't need to go right now, thank you!

Later, as they get older, my dogs will come and stare at me when they want my attention. When I turn to look at them, they will tell me they need something. Riker will stare, turn toward the door, and look back at me as if to say, "Follow me, Mom!" Bashir will nudge my arm, especially if I'm working at the computer. I will then ask the dog, "Do you need to go potty?" If the answer is yes, then I'll let him outside.

No Excuses!

Many Yorkie owners seem to be masters at making excuses. I don't know if it's because their dogs are so tiny, or so cute, but excuses are always readily available. "He had an accident because he ate too much!" or "It is too cold/hot/windy/rainy/snowy outside." Excuses, however, won't housetrain your dog.

Now, I understand that accidents happen. Perhaps you won't be watching the puppy closely enough and he will urinate on the floor. When an accident does happen, you must handle it very carefully. It's important the puppy learns that urinating and defecating are not wrong, but the place where he did it was wrong. If the puppy feels that relieving himself is wrong, then he will become sneaky about it, and you will find puddles in strange places, including behind the furniture.

If you come upon the puppy as he is having an accident, then use a verbal interruption, "Acck! What are you doing?" Scoop him up and take him outside. Then clean up the mess, but do not let him watch you clean it up.

Years ago, if a dog had an accident inside, owners were told to rub the dog's nose in his urine or feces; that would teach him to go outside! How on Earth would that teach a dog to go outside? Don't do that!

Yorkie Smarts

If you find an accident after the fact, don't correct the puppy—it's too late. Instead, consider it your accident; you weren't paying enough attention, or ignored the puppy, or didn't get him outside often enough.

Rubbing the puppy's nose in his mess teaches him that the urine or feces is the problem, and that's not what you want him to learn. Don't drag him to his mess and shake him or yell at him; that will only confuse him. Remember, the act of relieving himself is not wrong; it's the act of relieving himself in the house that's wrong. Make sure your message is very clear.

If your puppy is having a few accidents in the house, you need to make sure you're doing things correctly:

- Are you getting him outside (or to his box) on a regular schedule?

- Are you going outside with him (or to his box) so that you can praise him when he relieves himself outside?

- Are you limiting his freedom in the house?

Successful housetraining is based on setting the puppy up for success by allowing few accidents to happen, and then praising the puppy when he relieves himself where you ask him to do so.

Using Doggy Doors

Doggy doors can be very effective for larger-size adult Yorkies who are left home alone for many hours each day. The dog can go outside to relieve himself or to lie in the sun and can get back inside when he so desires. However, I don't recommend doggy doors for very small Yorkies, as they can be vulnerable to attack by larger dogs that might get into the yard, coyotes, or even birds of prey. The only way to use a doggy door with a very small Yorkie is to have the door open to a covered, secure dog run.

Dog Talk

A **doggy door** is a small door (or flap) that can be installed so that your Yorkie can go in and out as he pleases without any assistance from you. It should open to a safe, secure area.

A doggy door is rarely the right choice for puppies because the door eliminates you from the training process, and you are a vital part of it. You need to go outside with your puppy to teach him the command to relieve himself. You also need to praise him when he does relieve himself in the correct place.

I also don't recommend doggy doors for adult dogs who are not well housetrained. Although the dog may go through the door and relieve himself outside, he's not learning to control his bowels and bladder, he's not learning to relieve himself on command, and he's not learning how to tell you he needs to go outside. So he's missing several very important lessons.

In addition, if he goes in and out on his own, do you know whether he has relieved himself? If you're getting ready to take him for a car ride, do you know whether he has a full bladder or not?

Watch Out!

If you live in an area with hawks or eagles, don't use a doggy door unless it opens out into a covered, secure dog run. Never let your Yorkie go out to an open backyard without you.

Be Patient

All puppies need time to grow and develop bladder and bowel control, so be patient with your Yorkie puppy's housetraining. Just establish a schedule that seems to work for you and your puppy and stick to it. If you follow the right schedule, your puppy will do fine. However, the lack of accidents doesn't mean you can ease up on your supervision; instead, a lack of accidents means your schedule is good! If you ease up too soon, your puppy will have some accidents, and you'll have to start all over again.

A schedule that works for you and your puppy, along with careful supervision and lots of patience, will work. Puppies do eventually grow up, and all your efforts will pay off when you find that you have a well-housetrained, reliable dog.

The Least You Need to Know

- A crate will help your Yorkie develop bowel and bladder control.

- Teach your dog to relieve himself outside and on command.

- Establish a schedule for eating, sleeping, playing, and going outside.

- Be patient. Housetraining takes time.

Chapter 8

When Will the Biting Stop?

In This Chapter

- ◊ Remembering that puppies have sharp teeth
- ◊ Inhibiting biting is important
- ◊ Trying not to make it worse
- ◊ Teaching your puppy

Puppies bite. And sometimes those sharp tiny teeth can hurt, especially if the Yorkie puppy is overstimulated during play sessions. Although using their mouth is natural, it can definitely create some problems. Sometimes puppy owners make the situation worse, too, causing the biting to go on and on.

It's important that all puppies, even tiny ones, learn that using their mouth on people is a bad idea that will not be tolerated. After all, you would feel horrible if your Yorkie bit a guest, a delivery man, or a relative.

Biting Is Natural

Although sharp puppy teeth can hurt and even draw blood, it is very natural (and normal) for puppies to bite. And they bite for many different reasons:

- Your puppy doesn't have any hands and so manipulates the world around him with his mouth. That includes you!

- A puppy uses his mouth during play to grip and hold on just as he used to do with his littermates.

- He uses his mouth to protest things he doesn't like, such as grooming and brushing or trimming his toenails.

- Your puppy also chews and bites when he's teething (when the puppy teeth are coming in, and again later when he loses his puppy teeth and the adult teeth are coming in) because his gums hurt.

> **Watch Out!**
> If your dog bites someone, you can be held liable for medical bills, can be sued in civil court, and can potentially face criminal charges. And the size of the dog doing the biting doesn't matter at all.

Natural Doesn't Mean Right

Biting is natural, yes, but that doesn't mean it should continue. After all, there are many behaviors that are natural to people that we do not do in polite society! Biting is one of those behaviors that dogs do naturally but need to be controlled.

Ideally, your puppy's mother should have begun teaching him that biting is not allowed. Most momma dogs, when bitten by one of their puppies, will growl at the offending puppy until he stops biting and rolls over, baring his belly. In this way he learns that biting an adult is not tolerated.

Unfortunately, sometimes the owners of the mother dog do not understand what she's doing—they do not see that she is teaching her puppy—and they feel she is being mean to the puppy. They may then rescue the puppy—take him away from his mother—and cuddle him; which teaches him that biting ends up in cuddles! Or the owners may take the momma dog away from her puppies and then all the puppies are deprived of this important lesson.

If the puppy remains with his littermates until he's eight or nine weeks old, they can also provide a lesson about biting. During play, when a puppy bites too hard, the sibling will cry out, "Yipe!" in a shrill tone of voice. This normally stops the biting puppy right then and there. He learns, "Oh, if I bite that hard, it hurts!" This teaches the puppy *bite inhibition*.

Adult dogs other than your puppy's mother won't tolerate biting, either. Properly taught and socialized adult dogs do not hurt each other intentionally during play. If one does get too rough, he's apt to find himself alone as other dogs won't play with him. Or, in the worst-case scenario, a dog fight will ensue.

Dog Talk

Bite inhibition is when the puppy (and then adult dog) learns to control his desires to bite and the pressure that he uses with his mouth during play.

Bet You Didn't Know

Most of the learning provided by the mother dog happens after six weeks of age. If puppies are taken from Mom too soon—say between six and eight weeks—they miss these lessons.

Adult dogs will not tolerate your Yorkie using his teeth inappropriately, and neither should you.

When Does It Stop?

Unfortunately, puppy biting is not limited just to puppyhood. If the puppy was not taught by his mother or littermates to control his biting, then it's up to you, the puppy's new owner, to stop it.

There is no age where the puppy will "outgrow" the behavior. In fact, if the puppy doesn't learn that he shouldn't bite, he will continue to bite as he loses his baby teeth and grows in larger, stronger adult teeth! Then you've really got a problem.

In addition, biting is one of those behaviors that tends to be self-rewarding. In other words, if the biting continues to get the puppy what he wants, he will continue doing it. So if he bites at your hands while you're trimming his toenails and you stop trimming because you're tired of being bitten, then he's won and will continue to bite.

Don't Make It Worse!

Unfortunately, some puppy owners make the problem of biting worse. Petra Burke, co-owner of Kindred Spirits Dog Training, says, "It's very important that the puppy does not turn this into a self-rewarding behavior. Do not let him 'win' any situation with you when he uses his mouth against you." To continue with our example of trimming his nails, that means use one hand to close his mouth to stop the biting so that you can continue to trim his nails. Or have someone else hold the puppy, keeping his mouth closed with one hand, so that you can continue trimming.

Choose Games Carefully

It's very important that you spend time playing with your puppy. Play is good exercise, it's wonderful for the relationship you are building with your puppy, and it's fun. However, the games you play with your Yorkie can also escalate the biting behaviors:

- Don't use your hands to wrestle with your Yorkie, pinning him on his back, or otherwise making him feel that he has to fight you.

- Don't wave your hands and wiggle your fingers in front of his face, teasing him. That's annoying and he will definitely try to grab your hand or fingers.

- Don't play tug-of-war games right now. You can play these later, when he's no longer using his mouth, but right now these games teach him to use the strength of his jaws against you.

Play games that emphasize cooperation—such as retrieving games, hide and seek, and trick training—rather than games that are adversarial.

Yorkie Smarts

When playing with your Yorkie, keep the ideas of cooperation and compliance in mind rather than confrontation. You and your Yorkie should be a team—together—rather than fighting each other.

Do not play games with your Yorkie that will teach him to fight you; instead play games that teach him to cooperate with you.

Aggression Begets Aggression

If you are aggressive toward your Yorkie—in play or in training—he will be more apt to show aggression toward you. Keep in mind, Yorkies are Yorkshire Terriers and terriers are tough little dudes! Most terriers were bred to hunt vermin, to chase off predators, and to patrol the farm property. Most terriers are relatively small (although Yorkies are the smallest) and had to be tough for their size.

If you teach your Yorkie that fighting you is acceptable behavior, you will have a tough time in the years to come. He will fight you no matter what you want to do, and his fighting may well include biting. That's not the kind of relationship you should have with your dog.

In the next section we discuss different ways to teach your Yorkie not to use his mouth. Just keep in mind as we go through these different techniques that violence and aggression are not the way to do it. If you tend to get angry when your Yorkie uses his teeth, use this as a good way for you to learn anger management. Or, when you feel yourself get angry, just get up and walk away.

Several Training Techniques

It would be nice if I could show you one training technique that would stop all Yorkies—puppies and adults—from using their mouth. Unfortunately, there is no magic wand! Every Yorkie is different, with his or her own unique personality—and every Yorkie owner is different—as is each dog and owner relationship. There are just too many variables.

So instead, we discuss several different techniques that you can try. You may find that a combination of a couple different things works best for you and your dog.

Stop All Fun Stuff

The first technique consists of stopping all pleasurable activities—all fun stuff—the second your Yorkie uses his mouth. So, if you and your Yorkie are playing (and you're being careful not to fight your Yorkie during play) and you see your Yorkie turn his head toward your hand with mouth open, don't wait until he actually bites. Use your voice, "Accckkk! No bite!" as you move your hand out of reach. Then get up, walk away from your Yorkie, and pay no attention to him at all for about 10 minutes.

The fun stuff—play and games—are obviously rewarding activities. By stopping the fun stuff and by ignoring the dog for a few minutes, you're making his violence toward you (his biting) nonrewarding. Remember, in the dog's world the fun things (the rewarding behaviors) are the ones that will be repeated.

Yorkie Smarts

When you say, "No bite!" use a deep tone of voice much as a momma dog would have used when she growled at her puppies. Don't scream and don't holler; just sound as though you mean it.

Time Outs

If you find that your puppy gets overstimulated at certain times—during play or when the kids come home from school—give him a chance to calm down before he reaches that point. You can put him in his crate with something to chew on, and close the door to the room where he is so that he has some peace and quiet.

By giving him a chance to calm down before he gets overstimulated, you can prevent the biting from happening when he's too excited to think. If the behavior is stopped before it happens, then the chances of it not turning into a habit are increased.

Supervise the Kids

All play between the Yorkie and kids should be supervised by an adult. Let's state that again: all play (not just some or most of it) between the Yorkie (of any age) and kids (of any age) needs to be supervised (that means you're paying attention) by an adult.

Yorkies are very small, and although not as fragile as some other toy breeds, they are not strong enough to tolerate rough play or handling. Kids, even those who mean well, can be very rough. Kids can also be mean. Kids, when with friends, tend to like to show off and do things they might not otherwise do. Sometimes the dog suffers for that.

? Bet You Didn't Know

The Center for Disease Control states that 4.7 million people are bitten by dogs each year; with half of those being children. Kids between 5 and 9 years old are most at-risk.

By supervising all play, both the dog and the kids are protected and the play can be interrupted before it gets too rough. In addition, with supervision, the dog and the kids can learn how to get along better and what behaviors are allowed and what are not.

Stop the Bite

If your Yorkie is in your arms when he tries to bite—perhaps while you're trying to comb out a tangle in his coat—use the fingers of one hand to close his mouth. Don't crush his mouth closed—he is small!—but simply close it and hold it closed. If you hold him securely with one hand and arm, then he can't pull away from the hand closing his mouth.

You can use your voice to tell him this isn't acceptable, "Acck! No bite!" But otherwise stay very calm yourself and don't let go of his mouth until you feel him sigh and relax. If he continues to fight you, don't yell; don't scream; don't shake him. Just hold him and wait him out. Remember, aggression begets aggression.

When he relaxes, wait a couple seconds (to make sure he isn't just marshalling more energy) and then let go of his mouth. Do not say anything to him—especially no praise and no sweet talk. Let him think about what's going on.

Put a Toy in His Mouth

Many times dogs use their mouth just because it's there! They want to play; they want your attention; they want something but they don't know what to do! So they grab you as they would have grabbed one of their littermates. They don't mean to bite; they don't mean to hurt; they just have a mouthful of sharp teeth and you happen to be handy!

For these dogs, teach them to grab a toy instead. Every time you play with your dog, or when he appears bored, or when you see him acting antsy—hand him a toy, "Here's a toy! Yeah" and then praise him enthusiastically when he has it: "Good boy! Yeah! Good boy to have a toy!"

Then when you see him pick up a toy on his own, praise that just as enthusiastically! In the beginning, go overboard with praise. After all, you want him to think that having a toy in his mouth is the best thing he can do.

When he has the idea that a toy is great, then begin telling him to go find a toy on his own: "Where's your toy? Go get it?" And praise him when he comes back to you with a toy in his mouth. You can even teach him the names of specific toys and send him after his tennis ball, or rubber bone, or stuffed frog.

Consistency Is Important

Teaching your Yorkie not to use his mouth on people is going to require some cooperation from everyone in the family. You all have to do this the same way. If one person likes to play rough with the dog and doesn't mind getting bitten, then the dog will continue to use his teeth on everyone. He isn't going to bite just that one person. Perhaps a discussion of the repercussions (legal, ethical, and financial) could convince that person that this is important.

You must also be patient. This behavior is natural, so it's not going to disappear overnight. But with consistency, it will get better and your Yorkie will learn that using his mouth on people is something he shouldn't do.

The Least You Need to Know

- ☙ Biting is natural but cannot be allowed.

- ☙ Puppies should be allowed to remain with their mother and littermates until at least eight weeks of age (if not longer), as these are a puppy's first teachers of bite inhibition.

- ☙ There are several techniques to teach the puppy not to bite; try several to see which will work best for your Yorkie.

- ☙ The entire family must agree to work together to teach your Yorkie; there must be a united effort to stop the behavior.

Chapter 9

Socialization for Good Mental Health

In This Chapter

- ☙ Understanding socialization
- ☙ Knowing when and how to socialize
- ☙ Understanding fear periods
- ☙ Making socialization a lifelong adventure

Yorkshire Terriers should be, according to the breed standard, alert and self-confident. Yorkies are often called the "King of Terriers" because even though they are tiny, they have an awesome attitude that shouts, "Hey, look at me!" Unfortunately, the tendency of many Yorkie owners is to coddle and protect their dogs—especially puppies—and this creates problem behaviors.

A Yorkie who is protected from the world learns to fear the world. Everything becomes frightening. The Yorkie will be timid and afraid, shying away from noises, sights, people, and other dogs. A fearful dog also has the potential of becoming a fear biter. A fearful dog is not a happy dog.

Yorkies need to be well socialized to develop their confident, "hey, look at me" attitude. A well-socialized dog will be aware of the world, know his place in it, and know how to cope. A dog who has been coddled and overprotected will become fearful, timid, and shy. A dog who has been overly protected watches the world go by while a well-socialized dog participates in it.

What Is Socialization?

Dogs don't live in a natural world anymore; they live with us, with people, and although there might be another dog or two in the household, it's a human world rather than a canine one. Although dogs are born domesticated, they are also born with all their canine instincts intact, including the one called "fight or flight."

When any canine—wild or domesticated—is threatened by something that he perceives as potentially dangerous, he can fight it or he can run away (flight). When we *socialize* our dogs, we temper this fight-or-flight instinct; it's still there, but by introducing our Yorkies to the world around them, we make fewer things scary. We also teach our dogs how to meet new things so that instinct doesn't have to kick in quite so often.

Dog Talk

Socialization is the process of introducing a puppy to the world around him, and continuing the process with an adult dog.

The Importance of Socialization

Last year I had two Yorkies enroll in a puppy kindergarten class at the same time. Both had gone to their new homes between 10 and 12 weeks of age and both were 14 weeks old when enrolling in class. The similarities stopped there, however.

The first puppy, I'll call him Rover (to protect the owner's identity) had been coddled in his first few weeks at home. He was never allowed to walk outside unless it was to relieve himself. Rover's owner had never let him meet other dogs, even well-known, healthy, vaccinated dogs. He went to the veterinarian's office, his owner's office, and that was it. When he came to class, Rover was worried about everything, and when I told her to set him on the ground, he tried to climb up her leg to get back into her arms. As soon as I turned away from her, she picked him back up again.

The other puppy, Fido (again, name changed to protect the owner), was taken everywhere by his owner. He had already been for walks at the local harbor where he saw boats, heard boat motors, saw sea gulls and pelicans fly over-head, and where many people petted him. He had met the neighbor's healthy, vaccinated dogs, and played with a couple of the neighbor's grandchildren. When Fido came to class, he trotted in on the leash, visited with the other puppies, and wanted the puppies' owners to pet him.

Yorkie Smarts

Protect your dog from harm by removing him from danger. However, don't overprotect him; let him get to know the world around him.

Both of these puppies had been born with the terrier "devil may care" attitude, but because Fido's owner treated him as a dog (rather than a precious jewel) and introduced him to the world around him, he has graduated from puppy and basic obedience class, finished therapy dog training, and is now a certified therapy dog visiting people in nursing homes and hospitals. He is well adjusted, happy, and has the "hey, look at me" attitude.

Rover, on the other hand, dropped out of puppy class. He is still very fearful and rarely goes anywhere unless he's in his owner's arms. The groomer says she has a difficult time with him because he's afraid of the clippers, her scissors, and the other grooming tools. He has snapped at her on several occasions. His owner makes many excuses for him but has yet to admit that she caused her dog's behavior problems by not socializing him and by overprotecting him.

When a puppy is introduced to the world around him, he develops skills that enable him to cope with that world. When a motorcycle zooms past, a well-socialized dog may look, cock his ears, and then process that information, "Ah ha. I've seen those before," and continue walking. A dog that has not been well socialized may react with panic, pulling on the leash while trying to run away, or worse yet, he may try to slip out of the leash. He may bark and growl at the motorcycle, or react negatively to those around him because he can't get to the motorcycle.

> **? Bet You Didn't Know**
>
> The more a Yorkie puppy sees, hears, and smells—without being scared—the better he will be able to cope with the world around him as he grows up.

Socialization to the sights, sounds, and smells of the world around him enable the dog to become familiar with the world. He learns to think (instead of react) when things happen. He develops confidence in himself and trusts that you are there to help him.

When to Socialize

The best age to begin socializing your Yorkie is between 10 and 16 weeks of age. Yes, weeks! That is when your Yorkie puppy is becoming aware of the world outside of his family circle.

You must take the time to do this now; you cannot be too busy. If you don't socialize your puppy now, you will never be able to make up for it later because her personality, temperament, and views of the world will already be established.

Puppies develop at set times for the first few weeks of life and nothing we can do will change that. The puppy discovers his littermates during the third week of life and he learns to play during his fourth and fifth weeks. The breeder needs to be very involved with the puppies—handling them, petting them, and caring for them—during the sixth and seventh weeks of life, because the puppy is becoming aware of those around him other than his mother and littermates.

Developmentally, the puppy needs to begin socialization during the tenth and twelfth weeks because that is when his brain is ready for it. Studies have shown that if socialization doesn't begin during this age span, the dog will never develop the social skills he might have otherwise had.

> **Bet You Didn't Know**
>
> Your Yorkie's adult personality is shaped by both his nature and the nurture he receives: his breed and genetic heritage (nature), and his mother's care; the socialization and training he receives; and you (nurture).

How to Socialize Your Yorkie

Much of your Yorkie's socialization can be as simple as allowing him to meet new people. Take him outside and introduce him to your neighbors. Let him meet the neighborhood kids, the retirees down the street, and the teenagers across the way. Let him meet people of all ages, sizes, shapes, and ethnic backgrounds.

You can also plan outings so that he can go different places and meet other people:

- Go for walks to different places. Walk in a park, along the river, by the beach, and in the hills. Walk in housing tracts and in rural areas when possible.

- Many businesses are great opportunities for socialization. An ice cream store, pizza place, or even a tire store all have people coming in and out—most of whom will want to meet your puppy!

- Take him to family get-togethers. Let Grandma, Grandpa, the aunts, uncles, and all the kids pet him and play with him.

- Take him to the pet supply store with you. Let him meet the sales clerks as well as other customers, and then reward him by letting him pick out a new toy. In the pet store, he can also learn how to walk on slippery floors and see things he wouldn't see at home (such as display shelves and stacks of aquariums). He can also learn to walk next to a shopping cart—something that is very different!

🦴 Take him to the veterinarian's office even when he doesn't have an appointment. Just walk him in, have the receptionist give him a treat, and then leave again. That makes the vet's office something special instead of something scary!

> **Watch Out!**
>
> Don't introduce your puppy to every dog in town; be selective. Socialize only with healthy, well-vaccinated, well-behaved dogs who are safe with puppies.

It's important that your Yorkie puppy meet a variety of people when he's young so that he's not afraid of them.

See, Smell, and Hear

Introduce your Yorkie puppy to as much as you can; not all at once, of course, but beginning between 10 and 16 weeks of age and then continuing throughout puppyhood. Let him become familiar, comfortable, and confident about the world around him.

While protecting him from harm (without reinforcing fear) let him see, hear, or smell the following things:

- In the house:

    The vacuum cleaner

    The dishwasher, garbage disposal, and trash compactor

    The washing machine and dryer

    The hair dryer

    A plastic garbage bag being shook open

    A crumpled paper bag

    A broom and mop being used

    A plastic bag being popped

    A metal cookie sheet being dropped to the floor

    Children's toys, including some that make noise

    Balls of various sizes, shapes, and colors

- Outside:

    A car engine being revved

    The trash truck out front

    A motorcycle zooming down the street

    People (and kids) on bicycles, skateboards, and inline skates

- In the backyard:

    The lawnmower

    A weed whacker and leaf blower

    A rake being used

    The hose being shook out, untangled, and curled up again

    Water coming from the hose (but not squirted at the puppy!)

    Metal and plastic trashcans, including the lids

✎ Other pets or animals:

Big dogs and little dogs; hairy dogs and short-haired dogs

Cats

Rabbits

Ferrets

Turtles and tortoises

Horses, goats, cows, or sheep

✎ In addition, you can help your Yorkie by helping him do the following:

Walk him up and down some stairs

Walk him over a wooden footbridge

Walk him over a metal manhole cover

Take him on an elevator

Walk him on carpet, artificial turf, slippery floors, and rubber matting

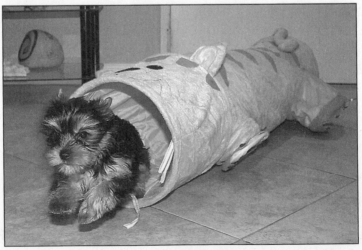

Socialization exposes your puppy to the world around him and teaches him that the world is fun.

Keep It Happy!

The key to socialization is to introduce your Yorkie to the world around him without frightening him. That means your tone of voice should be happy and upbeat; sound as though someone just offered you your favorite ice cream cone, "Ice cream!"

If your puppy reacts fearfully to something, do not "save" him. If you hug him or coddle him, or say "It's okay, sweetheart, don't worry," he'll take all that reassurance and assume you're praising him for his fear. In other words, you are telling him in human terms not to be afraid, but his understanding in canine terms is that he is right to be afraid. This is one of the most common mistakes that puppy owners make, but it's an important one that can have huge repercussions.

Watch Out!
Don't praise fear—even inadvertently—as that causes the dog to be more fearful.

To make sure there's no misunderstanding, be very upbeat. When something startles him, say in an "ice cream" tone of voice, "Wow! What was that?" and when you can, walk him up to it. "Here, look at this." Touch the motorcycle or the flapping sheet on the clothesline. Ask the child on the skateboard to come back and let your puppy see the skateboard. Ask the child to let the puppy sniff his fingers and then pet the puppy.

Encourage your puppy to come close and sniff the scary thing or person, and when he will, praise him!

What Not to Do

Don't try to introduce your puppy to everything all at once. Overwhelming him is just as bad as not socializing him. This should be a gradual process, taking place during the first few months of his life.

Watch Out!

You *must* control all socialization. Never let people get rough with your puppy, for any reason, even in play. If you think something is wrong, stop it. If you have to, pick up your puppy and walk away.

In his first week at home, especially if he comes home during the eighth week of life (during his first fear period—we'll discuss those in a moment), introduce him to things around the house. You can make sure he isn't frightened or, if he is, that you don't reinforce those fears. Keep things upbeat, happy, and matter of fact.

During his second week at home, take him outside a little more, introduce him to a few things around the neighborhood, and let him meet some new people. There are some things you must control, however, to protect your puppy:

- Don't let people—kids or adults—run around the puppy. This could be frightening or overstimulating. Plus Yorkies are tiny and can be easily stepped on.

- Don't let kids scream and yell while playing with the puppy. Again, this is overstimulating or scary.

- Don't let a bunch of kids gang up on your puppy. They can greet him one or two at a time.

- Don't let people grab your puppy and hug him too tightly.

- Don't let kids throw themselves on the puppy.

- Don't allow people to grab his face, put their face in his, blow in his face, or stare at him.

Remember, the whole idea is to make these outings fun and to build social skills, not to scare the puppy.

Watch for Fear Periods

During your Yorkie puppy's eighth week of life, he will go through what is called a *fear period*. At this age, he has become very aware of

San Diego Meet-Up Group.
Yorkie meet-ups are a great way to socialize for you and your Yorkie, too. Look for one in your area.

A puppy will trust you to take care of him for life.

You and your Yorkie will both enjoy going out in nature.

Bright eyes and a shiny coat are signs of a healthy Yorkie.

You can leave your Yorkie's hair loose or put it up in a barrette.

the world around him, and sometimes that world is scary. It's
important at this age that you try
to prevent frightening things
from happening, but if they do,
don't reinforce that fear. If you
do, the puppy will remain afraid
and that fear will stay with him.

Dog Talk

A **fear period** is a
period of time when
the puppy is more apt
to view things around him
as frightening.

More Than One Fear Period

Many breeders prefer to keep Yorkie puppies until they are 10 to
12 weeks of age so that this fear period doesn't cause ongoing problems later in life. If the breeder is dedicated to socializing the puppy
well, that's no problem. The puppy can still bond with you and your
family at 10 to 12 weeks of age. However, if the breeder isn't taking
the time to socialize the puppy, you would be better off bringing the
puppy home with you, watching for this fear period, and coping with
it and the socialization yourself.

Another fear period often occurs at four to five months of age,
when the Yorkie is losing his baby teeth and getting his adult ones.
His gums and jaws hurt, he's worried and often scared. Later, some
(but not all) Yorkies will go through another fear period when they
are 12 to 14 months of age. But this one is usually mild and very
brief.

Coping with a Fear Period

Yorkie puppies show they are in a fear period in many different ways.
Some will become cautious about everything; approaching things
(even familiar things) tentatively. Other puppies will be more selec-
tive, being bold about some things and cautious with others.

You can do several different things to handle fear. First of all,
talk to your Yorkie puppy in either a calm and matter-of-fact tone of
voice, or you can use a higher-pitched, fun tone of voice. Just don't

use a soothing tone of voice that he might mistake as sympathy; that will only reinforce his fears.

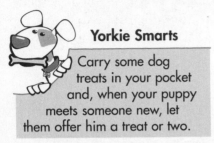

Yorkie Smarts

Carry some dog treats in your pocket and, when your puppy meets someone new, let them offer him a treat or two.

You can also try to distract your puppy by turning him away from what scared him; and when you turn him away, offer him a toy or a treat: "Here! What's this? Here's your ball!" Distract him and make him think about something else.

If the object of his fear is accessible, you might want to walk up to it, touch it, and show him it isn't as scary as he thought. Walk up to the motorcycle and pat it (as if you were petting it) and tell your puppy, "Come see!" If he walks close to it, praise him enthusiastically and tell him how brave he is! If he is really afraid, however, and plants his feet, don't force him up to the object of his fear. You can touch it, but let him sit back and look at it. When he's ready, then let him go up to it. If you force him, you may just make the fear that much worse.

Socialization Is a Process

Socialization is an ongoing process that's important for puppies, but it shouldn't stop just because a puppy has grown up. I'm always exposing my dogs—even my adult dogs—to different things. On any given weekend, we may play on the playground, go to a different park, meet a parade horse, or watch a marching band. My dogs have swum in the ocean, sniffed noses with a Budweiser Clydesdale, visited with Alzheimer's patients, and ridden on a San Francisco cable car. My dogs have hiked in the Sierra Nevada Mountains, walked through the forests in the Appalachian Mountains, hiked in meadows, and explored deserts. They have attended the county fair and walked in local Christmas parades. And they take it all in stride.

My grandmother always said that parents should raise their children to take the path they want them to take. Basically it's the same with puppies. Raise your puppy to take that path with you; if you like to do things and go places, introduce your Yorkie puppy to those things now, and when he's grown up, he'll be right there by your side.

Socializing Adult Dogs

Many dogs end up in local shelters or at rescue groups for a huge variety of reasons. Perhaps the dog was untrained and his behavioral problems reached the point where the owner gave up on the dog. Or maybe the dog's owner passed away. Unfortunately, some of these dogs may be unsocialized and may have behavioral problems associated with this. The new adoptive owner may have no idea until the dog begins reacting badly in certain situations.

Unfortunately, a dog who was not socialized as a puppy will never be able to make up for that lack. The age for beginning socialization is between 10 and 16 weeks and nothing can change that; that's the way dogs are. Although training should continue into adulthood, it has to begin when the puppy is young.

So what can you do if you adopt an older Yorkie who has not been socialized? Start the socialization process with him as you would a puppy, but have realistic goals. Understand that there may be some things he will be frightened of and that may not change. If he's never met larger dogs, he may not react well when he meets them. He may charge at the dogs or try to run away from them. Stop either of these behaviors, of course, and require him to behave himself but don't force your Yorkie to be friends with larger dogs.

Never force your Yorkie into a situation where he might panic and hurt himself or someone else. Rescued dogs often come with some emotional baggage; when you adopt one of these dogs you have to learn to deal with that baggage.

When Your Veterinarian Disagrees!

Your veterinarian will probably tell you to keep your Yorkie puppy at home until he has finished all his vaccinations. Until then, he may be at risk of picking up a contagious disease from unvaccinated, unhealthy dogs. In this chapter, however, I have just emphasized the importance of early socialization. Obviously, there is a disagreement here.

Your veterinarian is concerned about your puppy's health, and he or she has a justifiable concern. As a dog trainer and behaviorist, I am concerned about the serious consequences of a lack of socialization. Unsocialized dogs run the risk of developing severe behavior problems, including fear-based aggression. Granted, not all unsocialized dogs are fear biters; nor are all fear biters unsocialized. However, there is a strong enough relationship to show us that socialization must begin when the dog is a puppy. The other advantages of socialization are just frosting on the cake.

> **Watch Out!**
> Don't think that only stray dogs are unvaccinated or unhealthy; your neighbors' dogs may not be up-to-date on their shots or may not feel good. To protect your puppy, be forward and ask!

Protect Your Puppy

So how can you protect your puppy's health and yet socialize him at the same time? First of all, don't take him anywhere there are other dogs, especially potentially unvaccinated dogs, until your puppy has had at least two full sets of shots. These vaccines should include distemper, hepatitis, leptospirosis, parvovirus, and para-influenza. Most puppies have, at that point, good immunities.

Don't take him to places where there are large numbers of unknown dogs. Do not take him to the local dog park to socialize him; or a dog show; or the local beach where the dogs run loose.

However, you should enroll your Yorkie puppy in a kindergarten puppy class. Most kindergarten puppy classes will not allow puppies to attend until they have had two sets of shots, so the puppies in the class will be healthy. In the class, your Yorkie can play with the other puppies, meet the puppy owners, and learn at the same time.

Be Proactive

When you have a puppy, it's important to be proactive in ensuring your dog's safety. Be assertive when necessary, and ask questions of other dog owners *before* you let the dogs sniff each other: "When were your dog's last shots? Is your dog healthy?" If the dog owners get upset, too bad! It's your puppy's health, and you have every right to protect him.

Most of the dangers to your puppy's health come from unvaccinated dogs and their wastes. Keep him away from unknown dogs, and don't let your puppy sniff other dogs' feces and urine. Keep him away and pull him away if he tries to sniff.

You can keep your Yorkie puppy safe by being aware and careful, yet still get him the socialization he needs for good mental health.

The Least You Need to Know

- Take the time to socialize your Yorkie; its importance cannot be emphasized enough.
- Begin socialization early and keep it upbeat and fun.
- Fear periods are normal; just don't give in to them.
- Socialization should continue through puppyhood and into adulthood.

Part 3

A Well-Trained Yorkie Is a Happy Yorkie

In this section we expand on your training skills and your Yorkie's abilities. We show you how to teach your Yorkie the eight basic obedience commands and how to put them to good use. We also talk about some of the common mistakes dogs make and what to do about them.

Yorkies are busy little dogs, and living with busy dogs takes some time, patience, and ingenuity. We give you some tips on how to stay sane as you live with a busy dog. Some dog sports seem made to order for Yorkies. They love agility, thrive in flyball, and make awesome therapy dogs. We take a look at several different canine sports and let you know what skills your dog needs to participate.

Last we talk about Yorkie behavior. Why do Yorkies do what they do? After all, if you understand why your Yorkie scratches at your pillow and hides a biscuit under it, you can deal with it better.

Chapter 10

The Eight Basic Obedience Commands

In This Chapter

- Learning the importance of the basic commands
- Teaching those basic commands
- Using the commands at home and in public
- Determining tips for successful training

The eight basic obedience commands are Sit, Release, Lie Down, Stay, Watch Me, Come, Let's Go, and Heel. These commands should be part of every Yorkie's vocabulary. For pets and companions, these commands will help him be a nicer dog around the house and will make life safer for him. For example, when your Yorkie comes when you call him and walks nicely on a leash, he's a joy to take out in public. When he knows how to sit and stay, you can also teach him not to dash out through open doors.

For Yorkies who will participate in other dog sports and activities later, these commands are the foundation; advanced training will build upon them. Therapy dogs, for example, must sit for petting; they cannot jump on people—not even tiny Yorkies—as sharp claws could damage fragile skin. Dog sports such as flyball and agility use several obedience commands, including a good reliable Come.

Training also helps keep your Yorkie's mind busy. These are smart little dogs, and if not given something to do, they'll make their own fun. Training gives the Yorkie something to concentrate on, and that's all good!

These eight basic commands are useful in many ways at home with your dog. For years dog owners have told me what a joy it is to live with a well-trained dog, and I thoroughly agree!

Let's Start with the Basics

Many Yorkies spend a great deal of time in their owner's arms or on their laps. These dogs don't learn the basic lessons that most puppies, especially larger-breed puppies, must learn very early—the idea that their owner can control their actions. After all, when the Yorkie jumps up and down, the owner picks him up. When the Yorkie claws at a leg, the owner picks him up. It sounds as though the Yorkie has control, doesn't it?

With the basic obedience commands, your Yorkie will need to learn that you can set some rules, ask him to do some things, and he should cooperate. Some dogs learn this very easily, while others have a harder time with it. In any case, be patient. Remember, you are both learning at the same time.

Dog Talk

The eight basic commands are Sit, Release, Lie Down, Stay, Come, Watch Me, Let's Go, and Heel.

Now, before we actually begin training, does your Yorkie know his name? When you say, "Pumpkin!" (for example) does he look at you? For a few days before you begin training, have some really good doggy treats and some special toys at hand and, every once in a while, simply say your dog's name in a very happy, upbeat tone of voice. After saying his name, toss him a treat or a toy and praise him!

1. "Pumpkin!"

2. Toss the treat or toy!

3. Praise your dog in a happy tone of voice.

Pretty soon your dog will hear his name and turn toward you, waiting for something else to happen. And that is exactly what you want!

Although Yorkies are very small, training is still important for many reasons, including keeping his mind busy.

Teaching the Sit Command

Teaching your Yorkie to sit using the *Sit* command is relatively easy. Teaching him to sit still is a little harder, but we'll take this in small steps and set him up to succeed.

The Sit was introduced in Chapter 4. If you've been working on the Sit and your dog is doing well, great, continue on in this section.

If your Yorkie is a little iffy with the Sit, isn't sitting well on your first command, or just doesn't know it at all, then go back to Chapter 4 and review those instructions and begin training.

The instructions in Chapter 4 have you practicing with your Yorkie on a table or chair. When your Yorkie is sitting each time you ask him to, you can move him to the floor. Hook up his leash and place him on the floor in front of you. Stand up with a treat in hand, and ask him to sit. If he doesn't, tell him he made a mistake, "Acck!" and at the same time, move the leash (hooked to his collar) slightly up and back just as if your hands were on your Yorkie helping him. When he sits, praise him.

Teaching the Release Command

Your Yorkie needs a beginning and an end to each command. The beginning is his name. When you say "Pumpkin," he knows you're talking to him and he should listen. With the *Release* command, your Yorkie knows exactly when he's allowed to move from position.

With your Yorkie sitting either on the table or on the floor, tell him, "Release!" in a high-pitched tone of voice. Use the leash to gently move him from the Sit, and after he's taken a step forward, praise him, pet him, and encourage him to move. If he's hesitant to move, clap your hands and bounce up and down. When he dances with you, praise him some more!

Dog Talk

Release means "Okay, you can move now. You're done."

The primary purpose of the Release command is to let your Yorkie know when he is free to move from a previous command. This alleviates confusion; he then knows when he's done.

Teaching the Lie Down Command

Place your Yorkie on the table or chair, and hold the leash in one hand so he can't jump off. Have him sit. With a treat in one hand

and another hand (the one holding the leash) on your Yorkie's shoulder, tell him "Pumpkin, *Lie Down*," as you let him sniff the treat. Take the treat directly to the ground in front of his front paws. (Lead his nose down with the treat.) As he starts to move down, the hand on his shoulder can be assisting him in this downward movement. However, don't push! If you push, he may simply push back. When he's down, give him the treat and praise him.

Dog Talk

Lie Down means lie down on the floor or ground, and hold still.

When you're ready for him to move, give him the Release command. With the leash, encourage him to move. The Release from the Lie Down command should mean the same thing as the Release from the Sit command, "You're done now. You can move."

The Lie Down command is very useful, both in the house and in public. Use it in the following situations:

- Have your Yorkie lie down during meals so that he isn't begging under the table. Place him where you can see him but away from the table.

- Have him lie down at your feet or on the sofa next to you while you're talking to guests. He can't be jumping all over them or knocking their drinks over if he's being still.

- Have him lie down and give him a toy to chew on when you would like to have some quiet time to read or watch television.

- Have him lie down while you're talking to a neighbor.

- Have him lie down while you get your mail out of the box and sort through it.

When your Yorkie will lie down well on command, with a minimum of help, begin practicing it with him on the floor. Hook up his leash and place him on the floor in front of you. Give him the command to lie down, and if he doesn't immediately begin to lie down, reach down and take hold of his collar and move it down toward the floor, giving slight downward pressure. When he lies down, praise him. When you're ready, release him and encourage him to move.

Teaching the Stay Command

The Stay command is used with the Sit and Lie Down commands. We want your Yorkie to understand that *Stay* means "remain in this particular position while I walk away, and remain here until I come back to you and release you." The Sit and Lie Down commands by themselves teach your Yorkie to hold that position until you release him; but only while you are with him. With Stay, you will be able to walk away from him.

Dog Talk

Stay means hold this position until I come back to you and release you.

Place your Yorkie on a table or chair, with the leash on him, and have him sit. Hold your hand in front of his face about two inches from his nose. Tell him "Pumpkin, Stay!" while you hold his leash in the other hand. If he moves, use your voice, "Acckk!" and put him back in position. Wait a few seconds (two or three seconds in the beginning) and then step back to him. Have him hold still while you praise and pet him, then let him know it's okay to move by using the Release command.

After practicing the Stay command with the Sit command for a few days, try it with the Lie Down command. The training methods are the same except that you will have your Yorkie lie down. However, tell your Yorkie which action you want him to take. If you ask him to sit/stay and he decides to lie down, stop him and help him back up into a sit. He doesn't get to choose which command, you do.

Don't be in a hurry to move away from your Yorkie or to have him hold the Stay for longer time periods. It is very difficult for puppies and young dogs to hold still, and right now it's important that your Yorkie succeeds in his training.

Use the Stay around the house in conjunction with the Sit and Lie Down, as in the following situations:

- When guests come over, have your Yorkie lie down by your feet and tell him to stay. He cannot then be tormenting your guests!

- When you want him to stay away from the table while you're eating, have him lie down and tell him to stay.

- Tell him to sit and stay while you're fixing his dinner so he doesn't jump all over you and cause you to trip over him.

- Have him sit and stay at doorways, gates, and at the curb so you can stop him from dashing ahead and can teach him to wait for permission.

There are lots of uses for these commands. Just look at your house, your routine, and where you might be having some problems with your Yorkie's behavior. Where can the Stay command help you?

Teaching the Come Command

Come is a very important command—one that could potentially save your Yorkie's life someday. When I teach my dogs to come when called, I want them to understand that Come means "Stop what you're doing and come back to me right now, with no hesitation, as fast as you can run." This instant response might save your dog from a dangerous situation—perhaps an aggressive dog, an oncoming car, or a snake in the grass. Situations come up every day that could cause your Yorkie harm; a good response to the Come command could save him.

With your Yorkie on the floor with his soft leash on, hold the leash in one hand and have some treats in the other. Back away from your Yorkie as you call him, "Pumpkin, Come!" Make sure

Dog Talk

Come means your Yorkie should go directly to you, without hesitation or detours, as fast as he can run!

you back up a few steps so he gets a chance to chase you. If he doesn't come to you right away, use the leash to make sure he does. Praise him when he does come to you, "Good boy to come!" and then give him the treat.

Practice this also with a long leash. Regular long leashes can be too heavy for a Yorkie, so try a lightweight rope or heavy nylon (unbreakable) twine. Just cut a 20-foot length of rope and fasten it to your Yorkie's collar. Practice the Come the same way you did on the regular leash. Keep the command "Come" very positive as you call him, "Pumpkin, Come! Yeah, good boy to come! Super!"

The Come is one of the most important commands your Yorkie needs to learn, as it can potentially save his life.

As your Yorkie learns the Come exercise and is responding to it with enthusiasm, add some games to the practice. Call him back and forth between two family members and offer him a treat each time he comes. Make sure you keep it fun and exciting.

Watch Out!

Never correct your Yorkie for anything after you have issued the Come command. Timing is vitally important, and if he misunderstands a correction, he could learn that coming to you is bad and results in a correction.

If your Yorkie hesitates about coming to you—especially if something is distracting him—there are some tricks to make him come to you. First, don't chase him. That will only make him run farther and faster away from you. Instead, call his name in an exciting (not scolding) tone of voice and then run away from him. He will turn and chase after you!

Some other tricks will bring your Yorkie in closer to you. You can lie down on the ground, hide your face, and call him. Or bend over and scratch at the ground as if you're looking at something very interesting. Ask your Yorkie, "What's that?" in an "Ice cream!" tone of voice. When he gets up to you, don't reach out and grab him saying "Ah ha!" You'll never fool him again. Instead, continue to talk to him in an excited tone of voice as you gently take hold of his collar and praise him for coming to you.

Watch Out!

Don't call your Yorkie to come and then scold him for something he did previously. Not only are late corrections ineffective, but you're teaching your Yorkie to not come to you. Make the Come positive and fun all the time!

Teaching the Watch Me Command

Training your Yorkie can be very difficult if you can't get him to pay attention to you. Most dogs will focus on their owner at home, but when out in public, they want to pay attention to everything but you. However, you can help your Yorkie succeed by teaching him how to pay attention and then making sure it's fun for him to do it.

When you tell your Yorkie the *Watch Me* command, you want him to look at you, at your face, and preferably, at your eyes. Your Yorkie is to ignore the distractions and focus on you. Now, in the beginning, this focus may only last for a few seconds, but later, as your Yorkie gets better at it and as his concentration gets better, he should be able to focus on you and ignore distractions for minutes at a time.

Dog Talk

Watch Me means pay attention to me and ignore distractions.

To begin, go back to the beginning of this chapter and re-read the section about making sure your Yorkie knows his name. Practice that several times until you can get your Yorkie to wag the stub of his tail simply by talking to him. I want you to be able to say, "Pumpkin! Are you a good boy? Yeah! Such a good boy!" in such a happy tone of voice that your little Pumpkin turns into a wiggling mass of happy dog! When you can do that, you're ready to continue with this exercise.

Place your Yorkie on the table or chair, with his leash in one hand to prevent him from jumping off. With your Yorkie sitting in front of you and with treats in one hand, tell him with your happy voice, "Pumpkin, Watch Me!" At the same time, let him sniff the treat, and then take it up to your chin. This movement and position is important. Let your Yorkie sniff the treat so he knows you have it. Take it up to your chin (slowly) so that as he watches the treat, his eyes follow your hand to your face. As he looks at the treat and then your face, praise him with that happy tone of voice. After you praise him, "Good boy to Watch Me!" pop the treat in his mouth.

If he gets distracted and looks away, take the treat back to his nose and get his attention back to you. Remember your tone of voice.

When your Yorkie will do this on the table or chair, place him on the ground. Hook up his leash, ask him to sit, and have him watch you. If he doesn't, or if he does but then looks away, remember that voice. As soon as he looks back at you, praise him.

As your Yorkie learns the command, you can start making it more challenging. Tell your Yorkie, "Pumpkin, Watch Me!" in your happy voice and then back away from your Yorkie so that he has to watch you while you're both walking. When he can follow you for a few steps, back up in a zig-zag pattern, making turns and corners. Back up quickly, then slowly, talking to him all the while. Add some challenges. Make a game out of it and have fun with it.

Yorkie Smarts

Make sure you have a treat that your Yorkie really likes, and then save that treat just for training sessions. Keep it special!

Teaching the Let's Go Command

Good leash skills are necessary for all dogs. When on leash, the dog should respect the leash without fighting it, pulling on it, or choking himself on it. The *Let's Go* command will help teach those skills.

With your Yorkie on his leash, hold the end of the leash in one hand, tell him "Pumpkin, Watch Me! Let's Go," and simply back away from him. If he watches you, praise him. If he follows you, praise him even more. However, if he sniffs the ground, looks away from you, or tries to pull in the other direction, repeat your Watch Me and change directions so that he's caught off balance. When he turns to look at you or follows you, praise enthusiastically!

Dog Talk

Let's Go means follow me on the leash, keeping it slack, with no pulling.

Back away from your Yorkie several times in several different directions. Each time he follows you and each time he looks up at you, praise him. Every time he pulls away, sniffs the ground, or ignores you, re-direct his attention back to you.

Your goal is to have your Yorkie keep the leash slack as he follows and walks with you, paying attention to your every move. And when he does, you should praise him enthusiastically!

Teaching the Heel Command

When your Yorkie understands the *Heel*, he will remain by your side even if you walk fast, jog, walk slow, or simply amble. If you go for a walk through a crowd and have to zigzag through people, your dog should still maintain that position. The Let's Go command is a casual walk on the leash; Heel is more formal with a specific position.

Dog Talk

Heel means "walk by my left side with your neck and shoulder area next to my left leg, maintaining that position no matter what I do."

Teaching the Heel command requires a great deal of concentration on your Yorkie's part. Do *not* start teaching him to heel until he has been doing the Watch Me command for several weeks (not days, weeks!) and has been doing the Let's Go command very well for at least two weeks with regular practice.

Place your Yorkie on the floor on the leash. Hold the leash in your left hand and some treats in the right. Back away from your Yorkie as you tell him, "Pumpkin, Let's Go!" As he follows you, let him catch up with you as you back up slightly and turn so that you are facing the direction he is walking and he ends up on your left side. Walk forward together as you show him a treat and tell him, "Pumpkin, Heel!" Stop after a few steps, have him sit, and praise him as you give him the treat.

Repeat this several times, keeping each walking session short, enthusiastic, and fun. As he learns this command and is doing it consistently, begin making it more challenging by turning, walking quickly, walking slowly, and going different directions.

At this point in the training, with this method, always start with the Let's Go command and tell your Yorkie to heel as he arrives at your left side and you begin walking forward together.

After a week or two of this training, or when your Yorkie seems to understand what you want him to do, begin by having your Yorkie sit by your left side. Have some treats in your right hand, show him a treat, and tell him, "Pumpkin, Watch Me!" When he's paying attention to you, tell him, "Pumpkin, Heel!" and walk forward. When he watches you and walks with you, praise him enthusiastically.

This requires a little more concentration on his part, so make sure you keep the sessions short and upbeat, and praise your Yorkie's successes.

When you take your Yorkie for a walk, don't ask him to heel the entire way. Instead, go back and forth between the Let's Go and the Heel. Offer some variety and some challenge. However, when you start this training, do not let your Yorkie pull on the leash. Whenever he is on the leash, he is to respect it and never, ever be allowed to pull on it.

Tips for Successful Training

As I've already noted, your training will only be successful if you practice it regularly and use your training commands throughout your day. If the training is confined only to training sessions, your Yorkie will think it applies only to those sessions. Instead, use these commands regularly, both in the ways I've already suggested and in other ways that are appropriate to your lifestyle. After all, my daily routine is not the same as yours, so we will use the commands differently.

Don't be embarrassed to practice your training in public, too. If your Yorkie learns that you'll let him get away with bad behavior in public, he'll take advantage—I guarantee it! Yorkies are smart enough to figure that out. So make him behave, even if once in a while you have to give him a firm "Cut it out!" Just make sure when he does behave himself he gets plenty of praise, too!

Keep your training fun, too. If the training is serious and somber, neither one of you will enjoy it; and if you don't enjoy it, you aren't going to want to do it. Instead, have fun. Laugh with your dog, clap your hands and bounce up and down, and tell him what a wonderful dog he is!

The Least You Need to Know

- ✇ The basic commands are the foundation for everything you will ever teach your Yorkie in the future.

- ✇ Teach your Yorkie the eight basic commands—Sit, Release, Lie Down, Stay, Come, Watch Me, Let's Go, and Heel.

- ✇ Keep your training sessions fun and upbeat but under control.

- ✇ Use these commands everywhere; not just in training.

Chapter 11

Your Yorkie Will Make Mistakes

In This Chapter

- ✇ Why Yorkies get into trouble
- ✇ How dog owners cause problems
- ✇ What the common behavior problems are and solutions
- ✇ How to handle additional canine problems

Being very small has its advantages. After all, if a Yorkie jumps up on someone, he may scratch their legs or run their panty-hose, but if a Golden Retriever jumps on someone, he could potentially knock the person down.

However, tiny dogs—even Yorkies—can develop some annoying behavior problems. Sometimes the problems are not the dog's fault; many times the owner is at least partially to blame. So let's take a look at why Yorkies do what they do, and what you can do about it.

Why Do Yorkies Get into Trouble?

Your Yorkie jumps up on you because he wants your attention or to be picked up. As far as he's concerned, jumping up on you is not a problem. In fact, he's problem solving. He knows if he bounces up and down at your leg, you will reach down and pick him up. He has solved the problem of communication; he has taught you what he wants you to do. However, you may very well consider it a problem when he scratches your leg, or your grandmother's leg, or a child's face. You may also consider it a problem when he does it too often and becomes annoying.

We have to keep in mind when looking at problem behavior that these behaviors are not problems to the dog. Your Yorkie does things for a reason. We may not be aware of the reason, or we may not agree with what he's doing, but he knows exactly what he's doing. Sometimes, though, other things can affect problem behavior—occasionally quite significantly.

Is Your Yorkie Healthy?

Poor health or changes in health can trigger changes in behavior. A urinary tract infection or incontinence can cause housetraining accidents. An infected tooth can cause a dog to chew on inappropriate things. If your Yorkie has a sudden abrupt change in behavior, schedule a visit to your veterinarian before attempting to correct the behavior. Tell your vet what has happened and that you want to make sure a health problem isn't behind it. If your dog gets a clean bill of health, then you can look at the problem from a behavioral viewpoint.

Many dog owners assume any behavior problem is rooted in bad behavior, but most experts feel that at least 20 percent of all behavior problems—2 out of every 10 issues—have a health-related problem behind them. That's why it's so important to see your vet first, before beginning any *behavior modification* training. It would be very unfair to punish your dog for behavior caused by a health problem—behavior he cannot control.

Dog Talk

Behavior modification is the process of changing behavior. It combines training with an understanding of why dogs do things, and changing the dog, the owner, and the environment so the dog no longer behaves in a certain way.

What Does Your Yorkie Eat?

Some Yorkies will thrive on just about any good-quality food. However, dog foods that are more than 50 percent cereal grain carbohydrates are known to cause a type of hyperactivity in some dogs—including Yorkies.

Several other wise, good-quality commercial foods are very high in these cereal grains (rice, corn, wheat, barley) and, as we discussed in Chapter 3, this can cause some problems. The dogs affected by these foods can't hold still; they wiggle and bounce, jump and run, and are on the move until they're exhausted. They collapse, sleep, and then wake up to do the same thing all over again.

If you suspect a food-related problem, read the label of the food you are giving your dog. Make sure the protein is from meat and not from grains and cereals. Feed your Yorkie a food that doesn't contain a lot of sugar and artificial preservatives, colorings, and additives, either.

Yorkie Smarts

If you switch foods, take your time. Add a little of the new food to the old and gradually—over two to three weeks—add more of the new food.

Is Your Yorkie a Lap Dog?

Of course your Yorkie is a lap dog; that's why you got a Yorkie! However, don't forget Yorkies are terriers. They are active, inquisitive, spunky dogs, and your Yorkie needs plenty of time to act naturally.

Bet You Didn't Know

The amount of exercise needed will vary from dog to dog. A nice four- to five-block walk around the neighborhood would be enough for a Yorkie puppy but a one-mile jog or a three-mile walk would be better for a full-grown, healthy adult Yorkie.

When your Yorkie doesn't get enough exercise, he may be restless, act as though he can't hold still, or pace. He may even act depressed. A dog who doesn't get enough exercise during a long period of time may also develop health problems, including obesity, diabetes, and heart disease. An overweight dog is not happy nor is he healthy. Regular aerobic exercise can help use up your dog's excess energy and keep his weight at a healthy level.

Your Yorkie Needs Mental Stimulation

A bored Yorkie is going to find something to do to amuse himself, and you may not like what he chooses to do. You need to make sure you do something every day to keep his mind active and sharp; which in turn will help alleviate boredom. Try the following:

- Play games that make him use his mind. Play hide and seek (having him find family members by name) or teach him the names of his toys.

- Practice his obedience training regularly.

- Do some trick training.

- Get involved in a dog sport or activity so that he has something else to occupy his mind and body.

🦴 Increase his exercise so that he's more likely to sleep when left alone.

🦴 If he gets into trouble when left alone, give him a toy before you leave—a rawhide, a biscuit, or one of the new toys that dispenses treats as the dog plays with it.

🦴 Let him watch the birds at a bird feeder. You may be surprised at how much your Yorkie will enjoy watching the birds.

> **Bet You Didn't Know**
>
> I'm a huge fan of trick training. It's fun, wonderful for the relationship you have with your dog, and it's still training. Pick up a copy of my book *The Complete Idiot's Guide to Dog Tricks* and have some fun with your Yorkie!

Are You Your Dog's Parent?

In Chapter 4, we discussed how important it is that you maintain the position of your Yorkie's adoptive parent. As a parent, you are his leader and provide guidance for him, as well as affection and love. This is important because Yorkies lacking leadership can develop a host of behavior problems. Leg lifting, marking, mounting, humping, and other unacceptable behaviors are frequently seen. Aggressive behavior toward family members is common, as is destructive behavior around the house. Food guarding, toy guarding, and similar behaviors are also common. A Yorkie who doesn't perceive his owner as his parent or leader may try to assume the leadership position.

> **Watch Out!**
>
> If your Yorkie is an adult and thinks he's the leader and you are trying to change things, be careful. If you even think you could be bitten, hire a trainer or behaviorist to help you.

In your Yorkie's eyes, if you are not the leader, someone must assume the position! If you have not yet convinced your Yorkie you

are the leader, you need to change how he regards his—and your—
position in the family hierarchy. You can do this in a number of
ways:

- Play games that make him work for you; retrieving games and
  hide-and-seek games are good.

- People should go through doorways and gates first. You go up
  and down stairs first. Make him wait for you.

- Don't let him sleep in bed with you; he needs his own bed,
  although his bed should be in your bedroom.

- Make him sit for everything he wants. Give him one command
  to sit and then help him do it.

- Feed him at set times, giving him his food and taking it away
  after 15 minutes. Do *not* free-feed, leaving food out all the time.

- Think as a leader; be assertive and act confident.

How Do Dog Owners Cause the Problem?

As a dog obedience instructor, I watch dogs and their owners every
day. I watch how dog owners interact with their dogs and I marvel at
how well dogs get along in our world in spite of us. Unfortunately,
we—the owners of dogs—are often the cause of behavior problems.
And worse yet, the problems caused by the owners are the hardest to
solve because it's harder to see problems within ourselves than it is to
see the problems in our dogs.

Over-Permissive Owners

The most common types of owners I see with Yorkies are over-
permissive owners. Over-permissive owners want to spoil their
dogs and usually freely admit they spoil their dogs. Over-permissive

owners don't set enough rules or, when they do set rules, they don't enforce them. These owners are not the dog's leader, and many problem behaviors can develop as a consequence.

Over-Protective Owners

Over-protective owners are so concerned that something will harm their tiny dog that they don't allow the Yorkie to be a dog. By over-protecting their Yorkie, they take away his ability to cope with the world around him. By "protecting" him from everything, the dog often becomes fearful; sometimes aggressively fearful.

Bet You Didn't Know

Everything we do with our dogs causes them to react in some way. Watch your dog and see how he reacts to your emotions and moods.

Over-Demanding Owners

I also occasionally see owners who are over-demanding. Demanding owners would prefer the dog to be a furry robot that follows each and every order exactly as given. Dogs, of course, will make mistakes, and these owners will never tolerate mistakes. Yorkies belonging to these owners will never measure up no matter how hard they try.

Overly Emotional Owners

Overly emotional owners are quick to get excited or quick to react and often end up with dogs just like them. Unfortunately, during episodes of excitement, these dogs—especially reactive Yorkies—can get out of hand.

Your Yorkie isn't perfect; none of us are, and he will make mistakes.

Making Changes

As we have seen, behavior problems occur for a variety of reasons. Food, exercise, boredom, your reactions to him, and your emotions can all play a part; as can his health. Your household routine and how dedicated you are to his training also play a part in his behavior. There are so many different factors that lead to problem behaviors that trying to solve those problems can be challenging. However, it can be done.

So let's start at the beginning:

- Make sure your Yorkie is healthy. Don't assume he is healthy; make an appointment with your veterinarian, and tell your vet why you are there.

- Make and keep a regular daily schedule for training. Fifteen minutes of Sit, Lie Down, Stay, Heel, and Come—all on leash—will help keep his skills sharp and his mind attentive.

- Fun training is important, too, like trick training, so that you both enjoy your training sessions.

☙ Continue your Yorkie's socialization. Make sure he meets different people, new dogs, and other animals. An isolated terrier is an unhappy terrier!

☙ Play with your dog every single day. Don't just toss the ball absentmindedly while reading the paper; instead, get down on the floor and play. The time spent with you is important and so is your laughter!

☙ Make sure your Yorkie gets enough vigorous exercise; every day, summer and winter. Participate in this exercise with your Yorkie.

Yorkie Smarts

Preventing problems from occurring may mean limiting your Yorkie's freedom. Don't let him have free run of the house, and supervise him more closely.

☙ Prevent problems from occurring when you can. Put away the trashcans, pick up the children's toys, and put away the cushions for the lawn furniture.

☙ Teach the dog an *alternative behavior*. He can't dash out the front door if he learns to sit at the door and wait for permission to go outside.

Dog Talk

An **alternative behavior** is one that your Yorkie can do and be praised for that also prevents a problem behavior from happening.

Common Behavior Problems and Solutions

Yorkies are, luckily, nice dogs and normally don't have a lot of behavior problems. Most jump up, and because they are so tiny, that's not usually a problem as far as many owners are concerned. Some Yorkies are barkers, and others like to dig. We discuss all these problems and some others that are a little less common.

Yorkies Have Springs in Their Legs!

Yorkies jump up on people to be picked up. Your Yorkie knows that if he bounces up and down, looking really cute, and scratches at your leg, you will get the message and pick him up. You need to be aware that he is training you to do this, and you must stop the behavior.

Bet You Didn't Know

Teaching your dog to sit instead of jumping up requires consistency in training. Everyone must make sure the dog sits; if someone is inconsistent, the dog will continue to jump.

First, don't pick him up when he's jumping and scratching. Then, teach your Yorkie to sit. This may seem very simple, but when the dog learns to sit before you pick him up, or sit for attention, including petting from you, he will sit in front of you, quivering in anticipation of petting, and will have no need to jump on you. If you consistently reward him for sitting, the jumping behavior will disappear.

You will also have to teach him to sit for other people. Use his leash and simply do not allow him to jump up. Have him sit first (before people greet him) and then, when he tries to jump, use a snap and release correction as you tell him, "No jump!" Make him sit, and don't allow other people to pet him until he's sitting. If you have a hard time making him hold the Sit, use your rigid leash for this.

Barking

Yorkies are not normally problem barkers, but their high-pitched, shrill bark can be annoying. A Yorkie who is allowed to continue barking can become a problem barker, and that can cause problems with neighbors.

Start correcting barking in the house when you are close. Put some water in a squirt bottle. When someone comes to the door, for example, and your dog barks, walk quietly to the dog, and tell him,

"Quiet!" firmly but without yelling. Very few Yorkies like to be sprayed with water. When he stops barking, tell him, "Good boy to be quiet!"

If you yell at your dog to stop barking (most people's first reaction), you're doing the same thing he's doing—making lots of noise at the front door. To your dog, you're barking, too! So of course he isn't going to stop, he thinks you're the reinforcements!

Watch Out!

Use the squirt bottle on mist setting; not stream. A hard stream setting could hurt him if you hit him in the face or eyes.

However, when you quietly tell him to be quiet as you spray this water, he hears the command as you make it difficult for him to continue barking. Make sure you praise him for being quiet when he does stop barking so that he knows when he's behaving properly.

After your dog has learned what the word quiet means, start asking him to be quiet in other situations. Whenever he starts to bark inappropriately, tell him to be quiet, and make sure you back up your command. Again, always praise him for being quiet when he does.

If your dog barks when you're not home, you may have to set up a situation so you can catch him in the act. Go through all the motions of leaving: get dressed; pick up your purse, wallet, or briefcase; get in the car; and drive down the block. Park the car down the block and walk back with squirt bottle in hand. When your dog starts to bark, surprise him with a "Quiet!" and a squirt! If you set him up a few times, he will quickly learn that you have much more control than he thought!

Digging

Luckily, Yorkies are not normally problem diggers. Many will dig a small hole (usually in a corner or the garden) to bury a favorite toy or bone and some will dig a shallow hole to use as a nest. I usually recommend owners to allow these mild earth movements to happen;

they are usually not very destructive, and the dog usually keeps to the same place for a period of time.

If the digging becomes annoying, however, you can control it by giving him his own spot to dig. A kid's sandbox full of dirt or potting soil works well. To show your Yorkie that the sandbox is his digging spot, take a half dozen dog biscuits and stick them in the dirt so they are only partially covered. Invite your dog to find the biscuits and to dig there. As he finds the biscuits, completely bury a few so he has to dig for them and, in the beginning, help him do so. For the first few days, continue to bury something in his spot and invite him to find it. When he digs elsewhere, correct him and take him back to his spot; he'll learn.

Suggestions for Additional Canine Problems

Life is never boring when you live with a Yorkie, and that means Yorkie behavior can sometimes be unpredictable. You may let your Yorkie out in the backyard one day only to see him dig under the fence or try to climb over the fence. If (or I should say, when) your Yorkie decides to try something new, don't panic. Stop, think about what he's doing, and then follow the steps we previously outlined.

Here are a few suggestions for some specific behaviors:

- **Digging under the fence.** Bury some rocks in the holes he digs under the fence. Then try to figure out why he is digging under the fence. Make sure he's getting enough exercise, playtime, and attention from you.

- **Chasing cars or kids on rollerblades, bikes, and skateboards.** Keep him on a leash and when he tries to chase, correct him with the leash and have him sit. Enforce the Sit and Sit/Stay command. If he can't sit still, turn around, walk the other direction, and, if he doesn't walk with you, let the leash correct him. Praise him when he does walk with you.

🦴 **Barking in the car.** Have him ride in the car in his crate. It's much safer for him that way anyway, especially when the crate is fastened in with a seat belt. If he still barks in the crate, use the squirt bottle. Squirt him as you tell him to be quiet. Praise him when he stops barking.

Never forget to praise your Yorkie when he behaves properly!

The Least You Need to Know

🦴 Problem behaviors are not a problem to your Yorkie; they are very natural behaviors.

🦴 Problem behaviors usually happen for a reason. Try to find out why your dog is doing what he's doing.

🦴 Prevent problems from happening if you can; especially when you aren't there to teach him.

🦴 When you are at home, teach him what is wrong; and most importantly, teach him what is right!

Chapter 12

Skills for Living with a Busy Dog!

In This Chapter

- Asking yourself what makes a busy dog
- Changing dog and owner behavior
- Using exercise, training, and the crate
- Living with a busy dog

Sheik, a five-year-old Yorkshire Terrier, is a very busy dog. He plays hard with his toys, runs every morning with his owner, barks at anything that moves, and chases the family cat; all as much as he can. But in his busyness, he's also developed some destructive behaviors, one of which had his owner puzzled for more than a week.

One day Sheik's owner came home from the grocery store to find white fabric filling (the kind used to stuff cushions and pillows) all over the living room floor. Sheik still had some hanging from his beard so she knew he had been the destructive one, but she couldn't find where the stuffing had come from.

Sheik had chewed a tiny hole in a cushion at the end of the sofa just big enough to fit his small muzzle in so he could grab the stuffing. So for more than a week, every time Sheik was left alone, he would pull out more stuffing. His owner finally discovered the hole because the cushion had lost so much stuffing it was becoming deflated.

Identifying Busy Dogs

Kate Abbott, a dog trainer in Vista, California, defines a *busy dog* as "A dog mentally bright and physically active who has more energy than the average dog." Abbott has become an expert on busy dogs as she lives with one herself. Abbott says of her dog, Walter, a Cocker Spaniel and Poodle mix, "If I don't keep Walter physically and mentally tired, he's going to find something to do to amuse himself and I have learned through experience that I won't appreciate his efforts."

Yorkies have several characteristics that tend to make the breed as a whole busy. First of all, they are small but they are hunters. Given the chance, they will hunt mice in the woodpile and bugs in the garden. They are also very watchful and pay attention to everything that's going on around them.

Dog Talk

A **busy dog** is one who would rather be doing something, anything, rather than relaxing and tends to be in this type of mood a lot.

Petra Burke, co-owner of Kindred Spirits Dog Training, says, "Most Yorkies are a ball of fire! They are excited about the world around them, and they are very active. Yorkies are busy dogs!"

Changing Dog and Owner Behavior

Yelling at these dogs, using a leash to make corrections, or correcting them by other means will not solve the problems associated with an intelligent mind and energetic body. Instead, the owners of busy Yorkies need to look at their relationship with the dog first—with an unbiased eye—and begin making some changes there. After all, Yorkies are very cute and far too easy to spoil. But a spoiled, untrained Yorkie is no fun to live with.

Martin Deeley, a dog trainer from Monteverde, Florida, says some owners teach their dogs to be busy. He says, "Some owners don't allow their dogs to settle down; they constantly pet the dog, stroke him, hug him, and talk to him. The dog learns that his job is to entertain his owner and if the owner isn't initiating interaction, the dog begins to." These dogs constantly nudge the owner's hand or arm for petting, they continue to bring toys or balls for the owner to throw, or they may even begin barking at the owner for attention.

Changing this behavior isn't difficult, but does require consistency from the owner. Deeley, who is the Executive Director and Co-Founder of the International Association of Canine Professionals, says, "A well-trained dog knows when to go 'out of gear' and into neutral. Teaching the dog to chill out is easy by leashing the dog, then sitting on the leash or by putting a foot on the leash." The dog is restrained close to the owner but the owner is not to pet the dog, talk to him, or otherwise interact with the dog. Although some dogs will try to gain the owner's attention by various means, including nudging the owner and sometimes even jumping on the owner, most dogs will get bored and sit or lie down.

Bet You Didn't Know

Some dogs learn to work for negative attention. As far as they're concerned, yelling, screaming, and leash corrections are still attention, and negative attention is better than no attention at all. Make sure you don't allow this to develop in your relationship with your dog. If it already has, ask a dog trainer for assistance.

"During this process I use very little in the way of verbal commands," says Deeley, "If every time the dog gets up we speak to him, even to give commands, we are rewarding him by interacting with him. By keeping a foot on the leash, keeping it snug when he attempts to get up or pull away, and putting slack in the leash when he relaxes, we teach the dog to chill out when we do."

Watch Out!

Dogs who are constantly with their owner—in the owner's lap, in the owner's arms, or following the owner from room to room—are also more prone to developing separation anxiety. This is a behavior problem that causes the dog to panic when left alone.

Owners then need to learn to leave their dogs alone at times. Deeley says, "We don't have to keep touching them, talking to them, or asking to be entertained. All we have to do is watch the dog relax or sleep and smile when we feel like it."

Training as a Part of Life

"I am a firm believer that a trained dog is a happier dog," says Deb Eldredge, DVM, of Vernon, New York. "A trained dog who understands the Down Stay can be in the house with you, nearby, without being underfoot. Dogs also like to help, so you can have the dog carry things for you or pick up things." A dog who understands how to pick up things can take the dirty socks to the clothes hamper. The dog can get the morning newspaper or walk with you to the mailbox and carry home a magazine.

Training can begin with basic obedience training, which normally includes the Sit, Down, Stay, Come, and Heel, but it is especially important that for busy dogs, training should continue from puppyhood into adolescence and into adulthood. Dr. Eldredge says, "Most dogs hit the high point of 'crazies' when they are between 6 months of age to 18 months of age. Sort of like canine juvenile delinquents!" These dogs need training sessions that will occupy and tire their mind. The training should include obedience training but doesn't have to be limited to that; it can include advanced obedience training, agility for fun or competition, other canine sports, or even some trick training. Kate Abbott does trick training with Walter because it's fun for both of them yet can also tire him out mentally. "Walter probably knows 150 different tricks or commands—maybe even more."

A bored Yorkie will get into trouble, so keep him busy, make sure he gets exercise, and continue training him.

This training should not be limited to the training sessions but instead needs to be incorporated into the dog and owner's daily routine. Abbott says, "I had a private training session with a woman who had begun training her dog but was having some trouble. So I asked her to show me what she was doing. She began by placing some dog treats on the kitchen counter and calling her dog to her. He came and he performed all his exercises as she asked him to and did them quite nicely. So I asked what the problem was. It turns out that the only place she practiced the commands was right there, at the counter, and so the dog learned that was where he was to perform them. When they went anywhere else, he ignored her completely."

To prevent the dog from learning this lesson, practice all his training skills—obedience, tricks, or games—in the house, out in the backyard, out front, while on walks, and everywhere the dog goes with you.

Bet You Didn't Know

To use the basic obedience commands in your normal routine, have your Yorkie sit before he gets anything he wants (such as treats or to go for a walk), have him sit before he goes out a door or comes in one. Have him do a Down Stay Away from the table while everyone is eating.

Exercise and Training

A tired dog is a happy dog. Dr. Eldredge shares her home with several herding dogs, most of whom she says could fit the description of a busy dog. She says, "Exercise can consist of long walks and/or runs, depending on the dog, his age, and fitness level."

A walk around a couple neighborhood blocks might be more than enough for a Yorkie puppy but won't come close to satisfying the exercise needs of a healthy young adult Yorkie. In determining the exercise needs of your dog, take into account his age and his present level of fitness:

🦴 Young puppies and adolescent dogs need exercise in short sessions (10 to 15 minutes each) several times each day. Avoid too much repetitive exercise—such as running distances on concrete—as this can damage developing bones and joints.

🦴 Young adult dogs with no health problems can run, play, and exercise until they are panting, slowing down, and ready to take a rest. But if your dog hasn't had much exercise for a while, work him up to this point slowly; sore muscles are no fun for people or dogs!

🦴 Older dogs or dogs with a health problem should be examined by a veterinarian prior to beginning an exercise program. After a physical, your veterinarian can provide some guidance as to what your dog is capable of doing.

You can also combine training with exercise. Abbott says, "I combine training skills with exercise and play for Walter. I will ask him to sit and wait, then I'll throw his ball. He has to wait until I release him, then he can chase after the ball. When he brings the ball back to me, he is to give me the ball, placing it in my hand. I won't pick it up and throw it if he drops it to the ground or just spits it out somewhere in my direction."

Yorkie Smarts

Make self-control (and by extension, the ability to listen to the owner) a self-rewarding activity. The dog who has self-control and demonstrates it earns real-life rewards (going for a walk, playing ball, getting a toy).

Crate Training to Calm Your Yorkie

Teaching the dog to accept and relax in a crate is usually accepted as a part of normal puppy training as we discussed in great detail in Chapter 7 when we taught you how to housetrain your Yorkie. Crate training as a part of housetraining helps the puppy develop bowel and bladder control, and many trainers recommend that owners use the crate to help prevent destructive behaviors from turning into bad habits during puppyhood.

But crate training can also help calm a busy dog. Dr. Eldredge says that she has some household rules that all her dogs must follow, "Bouncing off the furniture is not allowed and wild games of tag are sent outside (to the fenced-in yard). However, if one or more dogs get totally out of hand, they might get a timeout in the crate."

The crate isn't a punishment; the dog is not being yelled at or thrown into the crate so he bounces off the back of it. Instead, he's quietly put into the crate, the door is closed, and he's given a period of time (10 or 15 minutes; maybe half an hour depending on the dog) to calm down. When he has relaxed in the crate, the door is opened and he can come out or remain as he wishes.

Abbott says, "Many owners will find that their dog may choose to go to his crate on his own. If Walter is feeling overwhelmed or tired, he'll disappear and when I go to look for him, the first place I check is his crate." The crate becomes a place of security as well as the dog's bed. For well-trained but still busy dogs such as Walter, it can also help them gain back their sense of self-control.

Food Dispensing Toys

Many times Yorkies, especially busy ones, get into trouble because they are bored. You may be busy with chores or work, or watching a favorite show, and your dog decides that he needs something to do.

Instead of having him chew a hole in your sofa cushion or torment the family cat, offer him a *food dispensing toy*. There are many different kinds available at your local pet supply store or in online pet supply catalogs. What all of them do is offer your Yorkie some dry dog food kibble or biscuits as he plays with the toy.

Dog Talk

Food dispensing toys are ones that can have food (such as dry kibble) inside or biscuits placed in holes in the toy. As the dog plays with the toy, it dispenses food.

By rewarding him (with the food) for playing with the toy, he learns that he can have fun while you are doing other things. You don't have to be the source of all his amusement. This is actually the same lesson Martin Deeley was talking about at the beginning of this chapter; this is just another way to accomplish the same result.

The toys that dispense treats or bits of kibble are wonderful for keeping a dog busy.

Living with a Busy Dog

Living with a busy dog can be a joy; these dogs are fun, always up for a walk, a game, or a training session. But it can also be a challenge. It's far too easy for a bright, intelligent, and busy Yorkie to create havoc in the household.

Far too many busy dogs—including Yorkies!—end up in local shelters and with rescue groups because the owner didn't realize the realities of living with a busy dog. But after you realize the busy dog doesn't have to rule your life and govern your actions, you can find some common ground where you're both comfortable.

Kate Abbott had no intention of getting a busy dog but now adores Walter; he charms her with his dark eyes, smiling mouth, and wagging tail. But she adds, "I can't ignore Walter's needs for very long. If I do, he becomes more reactive and will bark at the drop of a pin. He chews on himself and he'll bring me toy after toy after toy. He can't settle down. So I have to keep up with him. I make self-control a self-rewarding activity and I keep Walter's mind as tired as his body."

The Least You Need to Know

- Yorkies are busy dogs but the world should not be centered around their needs.

- Training is vital so that your Yorkie's mind is kept busy and so that he learns self-control.

- Exercise is very important. A tired Yorkie is a happy Yorkie.

- The crate can give the busy dog a place to relax, and food dispensing toys can keep him amused.

Yorkies Thrive in Canine Sports

In This Chapter

- ☒ Yorkies like to have fun
- ☒ Owners should begin with training
- ☒ Canine sports are great
- ☒ Meetup groups for Yorkies

As we discussed in Chapter 12, Yorkies are busy, energetic dogs with a very bright, inquisitive mind. They get bored very easily and need to keep both mind and body challenged. After all, a bored Yorkie may invent some games (destructive behaviors) you may well wish he'd never thought of!

Canine sports are a great way to keep your Yorkie challenged. In addition, they are great fun for dog and owner, and you may just discover a great new hobby as well as a number of new friends who share the same interest. I've met some wonderful people (and dogs) through my involvement with dogs and made some lifelong friends.

Canine meetup groups are a relatively new idea that has been made possible through the Internet. People who own a specific breed (such as Yorkies) in a specific geographical area (such as Northern San Diego county) post to the Internet, make contact with each other, and then arrange a meeting place. This is usually in a dog park or a dog-friendly park. The dogs can run and play while owners chat. It's a great idea!

Yorkies Just Like to Have Fun

Yorkies would rather do just about anything other than hold still. Sure, a snuggle with you on the sofa now and then is appreciated, but playing catch, chasing the cat, and hunting for critters under the woodpile are much more exciting.

Because of their temperament, personality, and active nature, Yorkies are perfect for several different canine sports. Not only do these use up some of that excess energy, but they also require some training and practice, thereby using that intelligent mind, too.

Yorkie Smarts

Check out the website www.dogplay.com for an overview of every dog game, sport, or activity yet invented!

You may find that you enjoy participating in one or more of these sports, too, as they are a great way for dog owners to meet each other. You will meet people who share the same sport (or sports) who also share an appreciation of dogs. These people may have Yorkies, too, or other breeds; but they all share a love of dogs.

All Sports Begin with Training

All dog sports, no matter whether they are organized sports or games you play with your dog in the backyard, begin with a foundation of basic obedience training. The basic commands not only teach your dog to do those specific skills, but they teach your dog to work with you and listen to you, and you learn how to teach him. All these are vital to successful (and fun!) games.

The exercises that your Yorkie should know well prior to beginning any sports, include ...

- **Come.** Your dog should not be off-leash anywhere outside a securely fenced yard until he will come when you call him every single time you call him, no matter what the distractions. Because not all dog sports are held in securely fenced yards (many are in community parks) that means you need to train very seriously so that his Come response is excellent.

- **Walk on a leash nicely.** Your Yorkie doesn't necessarily need to heel all the time, but he does need to walk nicely on a leash without pulling. He should never (read *never*) pull on the leash so hard that he's walking on his back legs with his front legs in the air. Not only is this bad for him, physically, but other dogs will read his body language as being rude. That, unfortunately, is how dog fights start. All dog fights are bad, but your Yorkie is too tiny; he could be hurt or killed.

- **Stay.** The Stay, in either the Sit or Down positions, are great for helping your Yorkie control himself. After he understands the game or sport he's going to participate in, you may find that he will anticipate the action and get overstimulated. If he will do a Sit or Down Stay, he can keep himself still and calm.

- **Watch Me.** This command, which focuses your Yorkie's attention on you, is very important in most sports. Your dog has to be paying attention to you when you give him a command—when you tell him what he needs to do—and if he's too distracted, he's not going to hear you or pay attention to you. However, if he can watch you on command, and focus his attention on you, there will be far fewer mistakes.

- **Leave It.** When your Yorkie is excited and distracted, the Leave It (which means ignore what you're paying attention to) followed by a Watch Me, will get him focused back on you.

? **Bet You Didn't Know**

Don't make excuses for your Yorkie's obedience skills (or lack thereof). Yorkies may be tiny but they are very capable and very bright; they can do all the basic commands and much more, and do them very well.

Ideally, train and practice the basic obedience commands prior to beginning any dog sports. Practice in a variety of places so your Yorkie learns to pay attention with a variety of distractions. When you are comfortable with your dog's responses, begin training in your new chosen sport.

Yorkies are bright, active, and curious and excel in many canine sports, including agility.

A Variety of Canine Sports

There are a wide variety of canine sports that your Yorkie can do. Some are team sports, where you and your Yorkie work with other dogs and owners and compete against another team. Others are individual sports, where you and your Yorkie compete against other dog-owner pairs. Still others are not competitive at all, but are just for fun.

Conformation Dog Shows

If you bought your Yorkie from a reputable breeder, he or she probably mentioned to you at some point whether your Yorkie was "show quality" or "pet quality." A pet Yorkie is a wonderful dog and there's nothing wrong with him, but it just means that in some way, he doesn't measure up to the breed standard for Yorkies. Perhaps his nose is too long or his legs are too short; it doesn't mean he's a lesser-quality dog—it just means he doesn't compare as favorably to the standard and probably should not be bred.

Dog Talk

The breed standard is the written description of a perfect Yorkshire Terrier. The goal of the standard is to choose the very best dogs for breeding so as to carry on the best traits possible. Originated by The Yorkshire Terrier Club of America, the breed standard describes the shape of the head, the length of the body, the color of the coat, and much more. For a copy, go to The Yorkshire Terrier Club of America, Inc. website at www.ytca.org.

If you don't know whether your dog compares favorably to the standard, talk to your breeder or go to a local dog show. Watch the dogs competing and afterward talk to some of the competitors. They may agree to take a look at your dog and give you some advice.

To compete in conformation dog shows, the Yorkie must have a full, long coat and cannot be spayed or neutered. A dog who competes successfully can earn his championship. A local kennel club or dog show club can help you get started.

Obedience Competition

If you and your Yorkie both enjoy your obedience training sessions, you may want to compete in obedience. It's great fun but it's very structured and the rules are very specific regarding what you and your dog need to do.

There are several levels of competition, from the basics in Novice through the very advanced when your dog would earn an Obedience Trial Championship. Dogs can be spayed or neutered and do not have to have a full, long coat. Nor do they need to measure up against the breed standard; that's only for conformation. Talk to a local dog trainer and ask if he or she does competition training, or look for a dog training club in your area.

> **? Bet You Didn't Know**
>
> Dogs can compete in obedience trials with the American Kennel Club (see the rules at www.akc.org) or through the United Kennel Club (rules at www.ukcdogs.com).

Rally Is Great!

Rally is a form of obedience competition but it's much less strict than regular obedience competition. You and your dog perform a variety of obedience exercises, from walking on a loose leash through much more complicated routines. But all the while, you can talk to your dog, encourage him, and enjoy the teamwork with your dog.

> **? Bet You Didn't Know**
>
> For more information about rally, go to the American Kennel Club website at www.akc.org or the Association of Pet Dog Trainers website (www.apdt.com/po/rally/default.aspx).

To compete in rally your dog can be spayed or neutered and does not need to have his long show coat. Talk to your local dog trainer for guidance in getting started.

Agility Is Fast and Furious

Agility is a cross between a speed race and an obstacle course. The dog and owner must work their way through an obstacle course, doing the obstacles in a specific order, as quickly as they can with as few faults as possible.

Yorkies, being small, agile, and swift, do very well in agility. The owners, however, must be quick themselves, able to direct their dog, and able to remember the order of the obstacles. Dogs may be spayed or neutered, and may have a short coat.

There are many different levels of competition, from beginner through very advanced, and several different organizations sponsor competitions and titles. Many trainers or dog training clubs have agility classes.

Bet You Didn't Know

For more about agility, go to the American Kennel Club's website at www.akc.org. Or check out the United Kennel Club's program at www.ukcdogs.com. The North American Dog Agility Council can be found at www.nadac.com and the United States Dog Agility Association is at www.usdaa.com.

Earthdog Trials

Earthdog trials were begun to help preserve the working instincts of small terriers. Because very few terriers are truly needed to control vermin anymore, terrier enthusiasts were afraid the small terrier breeds would lose their spunk and feistiness. In these tests, a rat is caged (to keep it safe) at the end of a tunnel. There are several levels of competition, but in the first one, the dog must go down the tunnel and show a desire to catch the rat. Dogs can be spayed or neutered and do not need a full show coat.

Bet You Didn't Know

For more on Earthdog trials, go to the AKC at www.akc.org or the American Working Terrier Association at www.dirt-dog.com.

Flyball Is a Team Sport

Flyball is a team sport where one team of dogs and handlers competes (races) against another team. During the race, each dog must run to a series of four hurdles, jump the hurdles, and then bounce against a wall which discharges a tennis ball. The dog must grab the tennis ball and then jump back over the hurdles to his owner. Then the next dog can go. This is a fast, furious, exciting sport.

Dogs competing can be spayed or neutered and can have a short coat. Various levels of competition are available, as are titles and championships.

> **Bet You Didn't Know**
>
> The North American Flyball Association can be found at www.flyball.org.

Dance with Your Yorkie

Musical freestyle is a sport that combines music, dancing, your dog, and trick training. You and your dog will dance together to music, working with the beat, while your dog performs tricks that work into dance steps. This is a sport in which dog and owner both have fun.

Dogs can be spayed or neutered and the Yorkie does not have to have his full show coat, although the long coat is definitely quite attractive in this sport.

> **Bet You Didn't Know**
>
> For more information, go to the Canine Freestyle Federation, Inc. at www.canine-freestyle.org. The World Canine Freestyle Organization is at www.worldcaninefreestyle.org. And the Musical Dog Sport Association is at www.musicaldogsport.org.

Therapy Dogs Provide Love

When I've had a tough day, there isn't much that makes me feel better than a cup of hot tea and a dog to snuggle with on the sofa. Dogs are warm, affectionate, nonjudgmental, and never tell your secrets to other people. Dogs are good for us.

There are several organizations that evaluate and certify dogs for therapy dog volunteer work. All require that dogs have a good foundation in obedience and be well socialized to people. Dogs can be spayed or neutered and do not have to be in full coat.

? Bet You Didn't Know

For more information about therapy dogs, go to Therapy Dogs Inc. at www.therapydogs.com or The Foundation for Pet-Provided Therapy at www. loveonaleash.org.

Yorkies make wonderful therapy dogs.

Yorkie Meetup Groups

Meetup groups are fairly new. People who share interests (types of cars or breeds of dogs) in the same geographical area meet via the Internet, and then arrange for real-life meetings. Dog owners often meet at a dog park or a community park that allows dogs. The dogs can play while the owners talk about their dogs. These groups are great for new dog owners, as the more experienced owners are always willing to share their knowledge. The groups also celebrate dog (and owner) birthdays, holidays, and have on more than one occasion celebrated a wedding of Yorkie owners who met at the groups.

The San Diego Yorkie Meetup Group helped the photographer for this book by posing for photos. Photos of many of their dogs are in this book.

To find a Yorkshire Terrier meetup group in your area, go to Yorkshire Terrier Meetup Groups at yorkie.meetup.com. Some active groups include:

- Atlanta, Georgia, at yorkie.meetup.com/301/

- San Francisco, California, at www.meetup.com/sfyorkiemeetup/

- Denver, Colorado, at pets.groups.yahoo.com/group/ DenverYorkies

Meet-up groups also often sponsor special training events, such as meeting at a dog trainer's agility course for agility lessons. Groups also often ask a trainer to come to a meeting to hold a Canine Good Citizen test, or a therapy dog evaluation. There are all kinds of fun things the groups can do.

The Least You Need to Know

- Yorkies are intelligent, curious, active dogs who need to be kept busy and out of trouble.

- All dog sports require a foundation of basic obedience training.

- There are several dog sports that Yorkies excel in, including agility, flyball, Earthdog trials, and therapy dog volunteer work.

- Yorkie meetup groups are great fun for dogs and owners.

Chapter 14

Understanding Yorkie Behavior

In This Chapter

- Understanding the canine body
- Understanding hunting dog behavior
- Looking at the strange things dogs do
- Learning common questions and answers about dog behavior

Have you ever wondered why your Yorkie does some of the things he does? Why does he sniff other dogs' feces? Why does your female dog mount a male dog? Why does he chase a shadow or the light from a laser pointer? Dogs can do some really strange things—at least strange to people—which can cause some misunderstandings. After all, most people get embarrassed when their dog tries to mount someone else's dog; it's not socially acceptable behavior to us, yet to your dog it's very natural.

In this chapter, we take a look at some of the behaviors that confuse people. We also discuss some of those potentially disgusting behaviors dogs do—such as eating cat feces! Sometimes we don't know why dogs do what they do—after all, they can't tell us—but we can make some educated guesses.

How Dogs Make Sense of the World

The way dogs perceive the world and how they behave has a lot to do with how they are built. For example, we use our sense of sight for information about the world around us. Some dog breeds, including greyhounds and other sight hounds, use vision but many other breeds, including Yorkies, also depend on their senses of hearing and smell for most of their information about the world.

There are also physical characteristics that make dogs react in ways we don't understand. For example, their digestive systems often compel them to eat things that seem strange to us. In addition, their reproductive systems exert powerful forces on their behavior.

How Well Do Dogs Smell?

We can't even imagine how well dogs smell the world around them. Our noses are dull by comparison. Their highly developed sense of smell is why dogs are used so frequently by law enforcement agencies to detect drugs, illegal substances, bombs, and even poached animals and animal products. The ability to smell is also important to the Yorkie's original job as a rodent and vermin hunter.

If My Yorkie's Nose Is So Sensitive, Why Does He Roll in Stinky Stuff?

This is another habit that puzzles many dog owners. Why would an animal with such a sensitive nose roll in cow manure, rotting carcasses, or other stinky stuff? Although the dogs can't tell us why, some experts say that many predators, including dogs, roll in filth to help disguise their scent. Other experts say that the dog simply likes a particular scent—for whatever reason—because not every dog appears attracted to rotting carcasses. Some dogs will roll in cat urine, some will roll on tobacco products, and others appear attracted to petroleum products. Some dogs don't roll in anything! It seems to be a personal statement that some dogs make.

Why Do Dogs Pant Even When They Aren't Hot?

Dogs pant to lose heat. A dog can lose a lot of heat through the evaporation process on his wet tongue. Because dogs don't sweat anywhere except on the pads of their feet, this cooling process is very important.

However, panting is also a sign of stress. When in a situation that bothers him, for any reason, your dog may begin to pant. If he anticipates something happening at the veterinarian's office, your dog may begin to pant even though the air conditioning is on in the office.

Why Does He Yawn When He's Not Tired?

Yawning when not sleepy is what is called a calming signal. If during your training sessions, for example, your Yorkie looks away from you and yawns, he is trying to tell you to calm down. Apparently, he is feeling stress, either from himself or from you, and he's trying to relieve it. Other calming signals include eye blinking, sneezing, looking away, and scratching.

Why Does My Yorkie Eat Grass?

For many years, experts believed that dogs ate grass to cause themselves to vomit, because some dogs do vomit after eating grass. However, most dogs don't seem to have any trouble vomiting and will do so whenever something doesn't settle well in their stomach, so that explanation doesn't seem to make much sense. Instead, it seems that many dogs just like some plant material, and fresh, growing grass is attractive to them. When given a chance, many dogs (including mine) will eagerly consume tomatoes, strawberries, apples, carrots, and many other fruits and vegetables, especially sweet ones. Although dogs are scientifically classified as carnivores, behaviorally they appear to be omnivores—animals that consume both animal and plant matter.

Does One Year of a Dog's Life Really Equal Seven Human Years?

No, that's not really true. A one-year-old dog is roughly the equivalent (mentally, physically, and sexually) of a young teenage human. After that, each year of your dog's life roughly equals about five to seven years of human life. Yorkies will usually live 13 to 16 years; sometimes even longer.

Bet You Didn't Know

The individual personal scent secreted by the anal glands is also why dogs smell each other's feces. That personal scent tells them who the dog is.

Why Does He Lick His Genitals?

Although licking one's genitals doesn't seem to be an attractive behavior from a human perspective, it is a natural action for your Yorkie. Cleanliness is important to continued good health, and your Yorkie licks himself to keep himself clean.

Why Do Dogs Smell Each Others' Rear Ends?

This is another behavior that people don't appreciate but is very natural to dogs. Dogs have scent glands on either side of the anus.

These glands, called anal glands, contain a scent that is unique to each dog. A small amount of scent is deposited each time the dog has a bowel movement. When greeting each other, dogs will take a sniff at these glands. Think of this as a personal perfume!

My Yorkie's Nose Is Not Cold and Wet— Is He Sick?

His nose should not be dry and chapped; if it is, call your veterinarian. However, a dog's nose feels cold because of the moisture that evaporates off the nose. His body temperature is actually higher than ours, so if there is no evaporation, his nose will feel warm to us.

Why Does My Yorkie Lower His Front End When He Wants Me to Play with Him?

When a Yorkie lowers the front end, including the head and shoulders, leaving the hips high, this is called a play bow. This body language is a natural expression of play and is used by dogs, wolves, coyotes, and many of the other canine species. Puppies will use this play invitation when they want their littermates to play with them, as well as with adult dogs and their human playmates, including you.

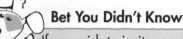

Bet You Didn't Know

If you wish to invite your Yorkie to play, you can use the same body language. Lift your hands high, and then bring them down in front of you, making a bowing motion.

Understanding Hunting Dog Behavior

Yorkshire Terriers were bred to hunt vermin, specifically mice and rats. They had to have a good sense of smell and acute vision to find their prey, and then had to be quick and agile to catch it. When the prey was caught, the dogs had to be tough enough to ignore any injuries the rats might cause them, and tenacious enough to kill the rats.

Today, Yorkies are still quick, agile, alert, tenacious little dogs. Movement of prey-type animals will still attract their interest and, if a rat or mouse happens into your house, it had better look out! Take care with small pocket pets in your home such as hamsters or guinea pigs.

Hunting dogs have certain behaviors and characteristics that can be confusing to some dog owners. Let's take a look at some of them.

When I Walk My Yorkie Off-Leash, He Sniffs Everything and Ignores Me. Why?

Your Yorkie is hunting. He shouldn't be off-leash outside of a safely fenced-in yard until he's trained enough to come when you call him even when he's hunting. Otherwise, leave him on a leash. If you want to give him more freedom, let him sniff and run on a long leash.

Why Does He Chase and Nip at the Kids?

He's reacting to their running and screaming. The kids' actions kick in what is known as the prey drive; the instinct to chase things that move and make noise. Because that is not how most children would like to play, and because nipping children is never acceptable behavior, you need to convince your dog that this behavior is not acceptable. Make sure the dog is supervised when the kids are playing and stop his chasing (and nipping) behavior *before* it starts. Use your leash to control him and use a verbal correction to let him know that he is not to chase the kids; praise him when he is calm and quiet around the kids.

My Yorkie Keeps Trying to Get into the Hamster Cage. Does He Want to Play?

I doubt it! A hamster is an awful lot like a mouse or a rat and your Yorkie doesn't understand the concept of a pet rodent. Keep the hamster safe from your Yorkie and never leave the two alone together.

Protect all your small pets from your Yorkie, including pet mice, rats, ferrets, and rabbits. If a small animal runs away, your Yorkie is going to want to chase it.

Why Does My Yorkie Lunge and Bark at Dogs We See on Our Walks?

There are many reasons for this. He may not have been socialized well enough to other dogs as a puppy, or perhaps he views other dogs as a danger. Yorkies can also be quite protective and may be trying to protect you. Last but certainly not least, as a hunting dog, he may feel he has to threaten the other dogs. Yorkies often have no idea how tiny they really are and how silly their threats are!

Dog aggression is potentially dangerous; a much larger dog may take your Yorkie up on his challenge someday and kill him. Therefore, stop the behavior before it happens. When you see your Yorkie paying attention to another dog, turn him away and get his attention on you. Praise him for paying attention to you and ignoring the dog. If you cannot do this on your own, ask your trainer for some help.

Looking at the Strange Things Dogs Do

Dogs do some weird things sometimes. We can guess at why they do some of these things, while other times even the experts are puzzled. Let's take a look at some behaviors that mystify many dog owners.

Why Does My Female Yorkie Hump My Friend's Male Dog?

Usually this means your Yorkie is just expressing dominance over the male dog. There are many ways of showing dominance, and this is one way. Very dominant females will often continue this behavior into adulthood, mounting subordinate males during playtime. You can stop the behavior when it happens if it bothers you, but it is normal and is not related to a sexual act.

My Yorkie Likes My Cat!

Many dogs—even hunting dogs—and cats live happily together, especially when raised together. I have three cats and three dogs and have had dogs and cats together for many years. When the dog is taught as a puppy to respect cats and not to chase them, the two species can live together quite nicely.

My Yorkie Eats Cat Feces!

Ah, the cat litter candy problem! Cats evolved to eat prey, the whole prey, including skin, small bones, meat, and guts. Commercial cat food includes meat but also contains grains and grain products that cats often don't digest well. Therefore, the cats are often passing through only partially digested food and, your Yorkie, smelling this, thinks this is a wonderful treat!

When he helps himself, though, and you get all excited, it becomes a *really* exciting treat; because, after all, you are excited!

Put the cat litter box somewhere the cats can get to but the Yorkie can't. Simple prevention is the cure here because you aren't going to change your cats' digestive system and the Yorkie is going to continue to search for kitty treats!

Common Questions and Answers About Dog Behavior

Yorkies are sensible animals and everything they do has a very good reason—to them! Let's look at some behaviors from your Yorkie's perspective.

Why Does My Yorkie Bury the Bone I Give Her?

Most dogs bury bones when they are through chewing them. Burying the bone hides it from other predators and protects it for future use. This behavior probably has its roots in hunting behavior; when survival depended upon what was caught during the hunt. Every scrap of meat or bone was important.

Why Does My Yorkie Still Pull on the Leash Even When He's Choking Himself?

Puppies aren't people, even though we've made them a part of our family, and they don't think like people. Your Yorkie is often so focused on going somewhere to see something, he isn't thinking about the discomfort on his neck. That's why we need to teach him to walk properly so he can go places without choking himself.

Why Is My Yorkie Constantly Jumping on My Legs?

What do you do when he jumps on you? Do you pick him up? He's training you quite nicely. He jumps on your legs, makes himself annoying, and you pick him up. That's exactly what he wanted. To stop him you need to stop picking him up when he's annoying, and then make him sit before you pick him up.

Why Does My Yorkie Want to Sleep with Me?

There is no reason why your Yorkie can't sleep in the room with you, but he needs his own bed. Not only is there a real danger of being squashed by you when he sleeps in your bed with you, but you each need your own bed. In bed with you, he will begin to think of himself as your equal, and he shouldn't. He needs to look at you as his leader.

Why Doesn't My Yorkie Pay Attention to Me When I Want Him To?

There are several things that could be happening. First of all, before you even start training, does your Yorkie get enough exercise? If not, paying attention to you could be hard. Does he get enough time with you when you aren't trying to train him? Playtime, time for grooming, and cuddling time are all important.

When you are training, use some really good food treats to teach the Yorkie to pay attention. Then keep the training sessions short and sweet so you aren't asking more than he can give you. Five minutes at a time is more than enough for most young Yorkies. With my dogs, I will train for a few minutes, and then play with them. Then I will train again for a few minutes and finish up with another playtime. My dogs learn that their concentration and attention is rewarded by playtime.

The Least You Need to Know

- Dogs do things for a reason. We may not understand why, but they do.

- It's important we know as much about our dogs as we can so that we can make both our lives more enjoyable and safer.

- Yorkies were originally hunting dogs and retain many of those instincts. This affects their behavior.

- If any behaviors escalate into aggression (toward people or other animals) it's time to call in a professional trainer or behaviorist for help.

Part 4

Caring for Your Yorkie's Health

The Yorkie's magnificent coat requires daily grooming and care. That long, luscious coat can easily tangle and matt, and requires some special skills to keep looking wonderful. We help you learn how to manage the coat.

Although keeping the outside of your Yorkie looking good is important, in this section we also discuss how to keep the whole dog healthy. Choosing a veterinarian you can work with is vital, as are regular examinations and vaccinations. We also talk about playing with your dog and daily exercise.

Last but not least, we talk about how to prepare for natural (or other) disasters as well as emergencies. Being prepared ahead of time is much better than trying to deal with a situation at the last minute.

Chapter 15

Grooming Your Yorkie

In This Chapter

- ✄ Taking care of that Yorkie coat
- ✄ Learning the grooming process
- ✄ Trimming toenails
- ✄ Cleaning ears, teeth, and more

This breed's luscious, flowing coat is a big part of what makes Yorkshire Terriers so unique. The blue and tan coloring, the long coat parted down the back, and the long hair around the face are trademarks of the breed.

This coat comes with a price, however; it requires quite a bit of care. Other health chores, such as nail trimming, ear cleaning, and tooth brushing, should become a part of your daily and weekly routine. As these become a part of your routine, your Yorkie will learn to accept them as things that happen regularly. This is much easier than fighting your dog each time you need to care for him.

With a regular routine, it's also much easier to keep an eye on your Yorkie's health because as you groom him, you can watch for problems such as ear infections, lumps and bumps, cuts or scratches, or fleas and ticks.

Ah, That Yorkie Coat!

The Yorkshire Terrier's long, flowing coat is a trademark of the breed, but it can also be a problem. That luscious coat requires daily care or it will quickly turn into a matted mess. *Matts* form most quickly where the dog's body moves: on the collar under the neck or behind the ears, the armpits of the front legs, and between the back legs. If the dog has an itch and scratches or chews, matts will form quickly in those spots, too.

> **Dog Talk**
>
> **Matts** are tangles of hair that become tight and almost solid. Often they cannot be brushed out and instead must be trimmed out of the coat.

Matts seem to have a life of their own. Some dog owners compare them to space aliens! Once a matt has formed, it seems as if its goal is to attract all the nearby hair, and get that hair to join the matt so that the matt can grow as large as possible as quickly as possible!

After the matt has formed, it becomes an irritant to the dog because it pulls on the skin and rubs against the skin. This causes the dog to bother it, making the matt even more of an irritant, and a vicious cycle begins.

Because matts are so unsightly, cause the dog so much bother, and often must be trimmed out of the coat (leaving a chunk missing from the coat), it's best to prevent matts from forming by brushing the coat daily. Daily brushing can catch tiny tangles before they turn into full-fledged matts.

The Yorkie's long coat can also attract debris. The silky coat makes it less attractive to debris than some other softer, more cottony coats, but it can still pick up twigs, burrs, grass seeds, and other debris during walks and romps in the park. Therefore, after walks and outside play sessions, and certainly at least once a day, check the coat for debris. If left in the coat, debris can cause matts to form.

Maintaining the Look

Many Yorkie owners find the breed's long, flowing coat a little more than they can handle. If you love the look of the coat but find it difficult to keep up with, there is a way to lessen the grooming chores yet keep the appearance of the coat.

Your groomer can help you make the coat easier to care for by keeping the coat on the top and sides of the body long and shaving it underneath. The chest, belly, inside of the legs, and groin area are shaved short. The top coat then falls over the shaved areas, preserving the look of the breed, but with easier care. You'll still have to groom your Yorkie daily, but you'll have far less hair to deal with.

Yorkie Smarts

Find a groomer you are comfortable with and then keep the lines of communication open. Talk to her. Tell her what you like and dislike. She can't help you with your dog unless she knows what kind of help you need.

If you think this might be something you would like, talk to your groomer. The two of you can look at your dog and decide how much coat you want taken off. It might take a couple of grooming sessions to get it right, but the coat always grows back, so if you don't like the cut, all you have to do is wait a while!

The Yorkie's long coat is gorgeous but does require some care to keep it that way.

Make It Shorter!

Yorkie puppies, with their shorter, softer coat, are very cute, and some owners of adult Yorkies like to preserve that look by having their Yorkie's coat trimmed. Although the shorter coat doesn't have the rich look of the adult Yorkie's long, flowing coat, the short coat is easier to care for.

Trimming the coat usually consists of trimming the longer hairs to a length decided upon between you and your groomer. Usually the coat is scissored (rather than trimmed with clippers) and may be from two to four inches in length. This gives the suggestion of the Yorkie coat but shortens it to a length that's easier to maintain. The coat is usually trimmed uniformly over the body, although some owners prefer to keep a little more length on the face to maintain that unique Yorkie expression.

I have seen some Yorkies trimmed very short—down to about an inch of coat or even shorter—and although these little dogs look quite athletic and spunky, they just don't look like Yorkies. However, some groomers have said that taking Yorkies down short is not as unusual as we might think. During flea season and hot weather, it's much easier to care for a short-coated dog than one with a full coat.

Busy, active people also find the short coat easier to maintain. Although a short coat isn't the trademark of the breed, I would much rather see the dog's coat short and well cared for than see a long coat that has been neglected.

It's up to you. What's most important is that your Yorkie is clean, healthy, and well cared for. So do what is best for you and your Yorkie.

Bet You Didn't Know

If you like a short coat, you can learn to clip your dog yourself. You'll need a good set of clippers made for dog hair (not human hair), a couple of different blades and blade guards for cutting the hair at different lengths, a book or video on grooming (several are available), and lots of patience!

That Gorgeous Showcoat!

Yorkshire Terriers who participate in conformation dog shows have long, flowing coats that drag on the ground. You can't even see legs or paws; just movement under the coat. That coat doesn't just happen; it takes considerable maintenance.

Because the coat can be damaged easily—even by daily activities—conformation show dogs wear their coat up in curlpapers. Curlpapers are those lightweight papers beauticians use to wrap around hair before it is wrapped around curlers. For Yorkies, the hair is not curled, but the curlpapers are used to protect the hair so it isn't damaged. Show dogs wear their coat up in curlpapers whenever they are not in a show.

Yorkie Smarts

If you think you would like to participate in conformation dog shows and would like to learn how to prepare the coat, talk to your dog's breeder. He or she can guide you through the process.

This takes a lot of work on the part of the dog's owner or handler, and patience on the dog's part. Instead of a flowing coat, the dog lives with a coat tied up in tiny bundles all over his face and body. Obviously, getting a dog ready for conformation shows requires some sacrifices, and this is one of them.

Most dog owners don't need to go through this with their dog; it's not necessary and is entirely too much work. Your dog can still be attractive and a good representative of the breed without that kind of sacrifice.

Grooming Is a Process

Grooming your Yorkie is a process, and it's important not to skip any steps. If you do, or if you try to rush it, you could end up with a bigger mess than you started with. So let's take this from the beginning.

Grooming Tools

The first things you'll need are some grooming tools. Make sure you have the following items on hand:

- **Shampoo and conditioner.** Use only gentle products made for long-coated dogs (or puppies).
- **Hair dryer.** Make sure there is a cool or low setting.
- **Grooming spray.** This is a spray that helps the comb go through a tangled coat. Your groomer can recommend a product.
- **Comb.** A metal comb with both widely spaced teeth on one side and narrow teeth on the other is great. You can find this at a well-stocked pet supply store.
- **Pin brush.** This brush has metal teeth with rounded ends. The teeth are often set into a rubber inset on the head to cushion the teeth.

- **Dematter.** This brush has three or four curved blades that are sharp on one side. It is used to brush through tangled hair.

- **Nail clippers.** Get a small pair of dog nail clippers. I prefer the ones that look like curved scissors.

If you have any questions about buying any of these items, talk to your groomer. I'll explain how to use these tools as we go along.

Brushing and Combing

Decide first where you want to groom your Yorkie. Although it may be easy to do this with your dog on your lap, sometimes it's really better to have an established place. When you do the grooming in the same place each time, your Yorkie learns what to expect and you can teach him how you want him to behave while you groom him.

I prefer to have my dogs stand on a table when I groom them. I can then stand and move around the table, or sit next to the table, all the while easily seeing the dog. I have the dogs stand on a piece of nonskid material sold as cupboard liners. It's inexpensive, can be washed easily, and most importantly, helps the dogs keep their footing on the table.

After your dog is on the table, teach him to stand quietly by holding him, talking to him gently, and keeping him in position. If he lays down, tries to jump off the table, or squirms, use your voice to correct him, "Acck! No!" and then reposition him while talking gently to him, "That's a good boy."

Yorkie Smarts

Teach your Yorkie to stand quietly as a training exercise. Ask your Yorkie to stand on the table, help him do it by using your hands to hold him, and then praise him after a few seconds and give him a treat.

When your dog will stand on the table, examine him. If there are tangles in his coat, get those out first. Work them with your fingers to see if you can pull them apart, then try the dematter. A little squirt of grooming spray sometimes helps. If you can't get the matt untangled, you may need to trim it out. Put your fingers between the matt and your dog's skin so that you don't cut skin. Gently, using tiny, tiny snips of the scissors, cut the matt out.

When the coat is free of matts and tangles, begin combing. Hold a section of the long coat between your fingers and comb the hair beginning at the last third of the length toward the ends of the hair. When the last third is free of tangles, comb the last two thirds of the coat, and then finally the entire length of that section. Comb the entire dog this way.

> **Watch Out!**
>
> Matts can pull skin tight, stretching it, so that when matts are trimmed out of the coat, the skin can be cut. Scissor cuts can be quite painful for your dog and may require veterinary care—including stitches—so trim with extreme care.

It's often easier if you begin in a certain order. Many people find it easier to begin at the dog's head and work down the body. Personally, I like to begin at the ears. I get all the tangles away from the ears and work backward down the body, and I finish with the face. I don't know why this works for me, it just does. As you groom your dog, you will find what works best for you.

When the dog is combed out, run the pin brush through his coat. This will smooth it out and your dog will enjoy the massage of the brush. As you brush, you can part the coat so it lies correctly. Begin the part behind the dog's ears and run it down the dog's spine to the tip of the tail. The coat should lie flat on either side of the part. Sometimes a small squirt of hairspray will help it lie flat.

The Topknot

The topknot is made from the hair on the dog's forehead. By gathering the hair together and forming a small ponytail, the hair is kept out of the dog's eyes. To make the topknot, gather together all the hair from the forehead. Divide the topknot from the beard at the invisible line from the corner of the dog's eye to the base of the ear. Hair above that line goes into the topknot and hair below that line goes into the beard.

With the hair gathered in one hand, smooth it by combing through it gently. Use a covered rubber band or hair band to hold the hair together. The placement of the topknot should be in the center of the head, equally between the ears and just slightly in front of them. A barrette, with or without a bow, can be fastened over the rubber band.

Don't pull the hair too tight; that causes the dog to scratch at the topknot. Also, once each day, before you groom the dog, take the topknot down and massage the skin of the forehead. Rub all the skin, making sure the blood is flowing well to the hair roots. This also feels good; when the hair is pulled one direction for a period of time, it can cause some mild discomfort and the massage will help alleviate that.

The Beard

The beard includes the hair under that invisible line from the corner of the eye to the base of the ear. It also includes the hair from the muzzle, including the hair from the top of the muzzle, which runs from the nose to the inside corner of the eyes.

The beard is high maintenance; more so than any other part of your Yorkie's grooming. The beard will pick up water every time your Yorkie takes a drink and will hold on to scraps of food after every meal. If your Yorkie goes hunting for mice in the backyard, the beard will drag in the dirt, picking up dirt and debris. In the house, it will find any dust bunnies you missed under the furniture!

Because of the beard's tendency to get dirty, it must be brushed daily. Begin combing from the bottom third of the hair as you did on the dog's body. When the bottom third of the hair is free of dirt and tangles, comb the last two thirds of the hair, and then the entire length of the beard. Part the hair in the center of the top of the muzzle from the nose to the middle between the dog's eyes. If brushing doesn't clean the beard, then you'll need to wash it.

The beard can grow quite long. In a conformation show dog, it can actually reach the floor! Most pet owners don't want to mess with this much beard, however, as it takes considerable maintenance. As your dog's coat grows, decide how much you are willing to maintain, and then keep the excess trimmed. Many Yorkie owners find a four- to six-inch beard fine. It's long enough to maintain the breed's expression but short enough to keep clean.

The Back End

Most groomers recommend trimming the hair around the anus to help keep the dog clean. If the coat is too long, feces can get caught in it, making a horrible mess. After your dog is thoroughly combed and brushed, use your scissors to very carefully trim the coat away from the anus. Just as when you trimmed matts, keep your fingers between the dog's skin and the scissors so that you don't cut the dog.

How much you trim is up to you. I suggest you trim just a little initially. After all, you can always trim more, but if you trim too much, you can't glue it back on (although it will grow back eventually). And if you trim too much, your dog could look really funny!

I also trim around my dog's genitals just to help keep things clean. For the boys, I trim the hair around the scrotum and penis sheath, especially at the head of the sheath. The hair on the end of the sheath can grow quite long and collect urine, looking horrible, smelling worse, and making the area susceptible to bacterial infections. For the girls, I trim the hair around the vulva.

Shampooing the Coat

Always comb out your Yorkie's coat thoroughly before bathing him. If you bathe him with tangles in the coat, those tangles will get worse. In fact, it will be as if you Super Glued them together! So thoroughly comb through the coat, getting out all the tangles.

Yorkies are small enough to bathe in a sink, and that's usually the easiest place to do it. Leaning over a tub can be tough on the back, and they are too tiny to bathe outside under the hose! A rubber-backed bath matt on the bottom of the sink can help him keep his footing.

Before you put your Yorkie in the sink, have a couple of towels ready, plus both the shampoo and conditioner. Put a cotton ball in each of his ears to keep the water out, set the water to a nice comfortable temperature (test it on your wrist just as you would for a baby), and lift him into the sink. Use a calm voice to encourage him to be still, and try not to let him fight you.

Thoroughly wet him and then turn the water off. Work the shampoo into his coat, making sure to get the shampoo down to the skin. Rinse him off, working from his head to his tail and then underneath him. Make sure all the soap is rinsed out. Then, work in the conditioner according to the manufacturer's directions and rinse it out.

When he is thoroughly rinsed, towel him off and wrap him in a towel for a few minutes. Cuddle him while the towel absorbs some more moisture and he warms up a little.

Blow Drying the Coat

Blow drying the coat serves a couple purposes. First, you can dry the coat while you brush it out, preventing any tangles from forming in the wet coat. In addition, you can keep your Yorkie from getting chilled while he's wet.

Unfortunately, many Yorkies don't like the hair dryer and fight it. It's important to introduce it to your Yorkie gradually and in a positive way. Bring out the hair dryer on a day when you have no intention of bathing your dog. Have a favorite dog toy at hand and a few dog treats. Sit on the floor with your dog and place the hair dryer on the floor, but don't turn it on. Ignore the hair dryer and encourage your dog to come close for the toy or treat. Play with your dog for a few minutes, letting him come close to the hair dryer, but while he does, don't touch the dryer. Just ignore it. Later, repeat these steps, but touch the dryer and move it. Continue this gradual introduction until you can turn the dryer on and let it blow toward him while you continue making a game out of the whole thing.

When your Yorkie will not panic with the blow dryer turned on him, you can then teach him to accept it while you dry him after a bath. With a couple towels under him, place him on the table where you groom him. Set the blow dryer on low and begin blowing the coat as you brush it with the pin brush. Blow and brush from the dog's body toward the end of the hairs. When the dog is entirely dry, finish him by brushing him all over, parting the coat and doing his topknot.

Grooming Challenges

If your Yorkie gets into oil, chewing gum, or gets sprayed by a skunk, a normal bath isn't going to solve the problem. Here are some suggestions for some special grooming challenges:

- **Burrs, foxtails, and grass seeds.** These can often be picked out with your fingers or combed out with the metal comb. If they have caused a matt, a dab of hair conditioner or a drop or two of vegetable oil may ease them out. If the seed is in a bad matt, trim the whole thing (seed and matt) out.

- **Gum and other sticky stuff.** Use an ice cube to freeze it and break it out. If that doesn't work, use some hair conditioner or vegetable oil to ooze it out. If neither of these techniques work, trim it out.

- **Oil.** Joy dish soap will usually cut the oil. Just make sure you rinse the soap out thoroughly.

- **Paint.** Do not use paint solvents; they are toxic. Try to wash the paint out, and if that doesn't work, trim away the painted hair.

- **Skunks.** Tomato sauce rubbed into the coat and then washed out will help dull the smell. Several commercial products specifically for skunk smell are also available; check at your pet store.

Touch Him!

One problem that many groomers complain about is that young dogs have not been taught to let people touch them all over. To make grooming easier for you and your groomer, make this a part of your daily routine. With your Yorkie on your lap, begin giving him a gentle massage. Start at his head and touch around his eyes, rubbing the lids gently, working down the muscle to his mouth. Touch his nose. Open his mouth and touch his teeth and gums. Massage around his ears, down the neck to his shoulders and back. Continue in this way until you have massaged the entire dog, missing no parts of him.

Yorkie Smarts

If your Yorkie comes up with something original and unusual in his coat and you don't know how to handle it, call his groomer or veterinarian.

This exercise will not only make it easier for you and your groomer to take care of your dog, but your veterinarian will love it, too. It's much easier to examine and treat a dog who is used to being handled than one who is leery of being touched.

Taking care of your dog's teeth, ears, and toenails also means teaching your dog to accept this personal handling.

Trimming Toenails

Trimming your Yorkie's toenails shouldn't be a stressful procedure, although many dogs turn it into one. If it's a part of your normal grooming, just as trimming your nails is a part of yours, you can eliminate a great deal of stress.

If you haven't bought a pair of toenail clippers, go ahead and get a pair. I prefer the kind that look like weird scissors with curved blades. You use them as scissors, too. I find these easy to use and the nail is very easy to see when trimming.

Have your Yorkie lie down in your lap or on your grooming table and take one paw in your hand. Pull the hairs back from around one toe and toenail. The nail is slightly curved over the quick but, once past the quick, becomes more slender and curves more sharply. You can see where the quick ends under the nail. The underside of the nail under the quick will be almost flat. Past the quick, the underside of the nail looks almost hollow.

> **Watch Out!**
>
> If you hit the quick and the nail is bleeding, rub the nail along a bar of soap. The soap will clog the nail until a clot forms.

> **Yorkie Smarts**
>
> If your Yorkie is worried while you trim his nails, take a little peanut butter and pop it into his mouth to occupy him.

Trim the nail slightly beyond the quick. If you cut into the quick it will hurt, your dog will cry, and the nail will bleed.

If your dog is very sensitive about his nails, just trim one paw at a time, take a break, and do another paw later or the next day. Don't try to do all four paws and turn it into a raging battle. That will only make things worse.

If you hate trimming nails and are worried about hurting your dog, most groomers will trim nails for a very reasonable cost. If you have your groomer do it, however, make sure you visit regularly—every other week at a minimum—weekly is best. Nails grow very quickly and nails that are too long will hurt your Yorkie's feet.

Bet You Didn't Know

When your Yorkie is standing upright on all four paws, his nails should not touch the floor. You may hear them clicking when he's running, but they should not touch the floor when he is standing still. If they do, they need to be trimmed.

Ears, Teeth, and More

Besides keeping your Yorkie's coat tangle-free and clean and his nails trimmed, you'll also need to keep his ears and teeth clean and make sure his anal glands are expressed regularly. All of these are less than pleasant chores to some dog owners, but they are necessary and, when you make a habit of them, they really aren't as bad as they sound.

Cleaning the Ears

To clean the ears, you'll need a few cotton balls and some witch hazel or a commercial ear cleaning solution. Dampen a cotton ball, squeezing out most of the moisture, and while gently holding the ear flap, wipe the inside of the ear. Make sure to get into all the folds and creases. Don't try to go deep within the ear; just clean what is easily reachable. If the ear is dirty, use two or three cotton balls.

If the ears are very dirty, have a lot of matter in them, smell bad, and the skin is red and hot, your dog has an ear infection. Make a veterinary appointment as soon as you can; these can be painful and will not get better without treatment.

The ears need to be cleaned at least once a week, but if you find that your dog's ears get dirty, twice a week cleaning is fine.

Cleaning Teeth

Dogs need their teeth cleaned just as we do. When the teeth are dirty, bacteria builds up and the mouth becomes diseased. A dirty mouth can also lead to other health problems. We know now that bacteria from a dirty mouth can affect the dog's heart, liver, and kidneys; sometimes quite seriously.

Watch Out!

Don't use toothpaste made for people. Not all the ingredients are safe for dogs and most dogs dislike the taste.

A child's battery powered toothbrush will work well for your Yorkie, along with toothpaste made specifically for dogs or, if your dog keeps trying to eat that toothpaste, you can use plain baking soda mixed with enough water to form a paste.

When you begin brushing your Yorkie's teeth, do so very gradually. Rub a few times on one spot in the mouth and then stop. Praise your dog, make a fuss over him, and then repeat it. Come back later and do some more. In the beginning, don't try to brush all his teeth thoroughly. Instead, get him used to it gradually so he doesn't fight you.

If his gums are very red and bleed, or if he has a broken tooth, or a buildup of plaque on his teeth, your dog will need veterinary care before you work on his teeth.

What Are Anal Glands?

The anal glands are small glands found on each side of the anus. As the dog relieves himself, small amounts of the oil produced in those glands are squeezed out with the feces. This oil is individual to each dog and is one reason why dogs smell each others' feces.

Sometimes, especially when stools are soft or when the glands produce too much oil, the glands become full. This causes pressure and irritation. Many dogs will at this point drag their rear on the ground, scratching the glands and trying to relieve the irritation. Unfortunately, this dragging can get dirt into the glands and cause even more irritation, sometimes to the point of serious infections.

Groomers often routinely express anal glands during grooming, especially if a particular dog is known to have a problem. However, because many dogs express their glands normally, this should not be done unless your veterinarian rec- ommends it. During your dog's next visit to the vet, or if your dog seems to have an irritated anus, ask about the anal glands. If your veterinarian seems to think it's warranted, he or she may show you how to check the anal glands, and if needed, how to express them.

Bet You Didn't Know

If your dog is sud- denly startled and produces a strong, offensive odor and you find a few dark brown oily spots, that is oil from the anal glands.

The Least You Need to Know

- The Yorkie's wonderful coat needs special care.

- If caring for the long coat is too much for you, a Yorkie with a haircut is still an attractive dog and a wonderful pet.

- Grooming is a process and should be done regularly.

- Trimming toenails doesn't have to be stressful.

- Cleaning your Yorkie's ears, brushing his teeth, and checking his anal glands should be a part of your dog's regular grooming care.

Chapter 16

Keeping Your Yorkie Healthy

In This Chapter

- Finding and working with your veterinarian
- Spaying and neutering your dog
- Taking care of your Yorkie
- Realizing the importance and fun of exercise and playtime

Yorkies are, as a general rule, hardy, healthy little dogs. They can't maintain this good health by themselves, however. Your care is vital to their ongoing good health, as is your veterinarian's knowledge, help, and care. Between the two of you, you can help your Yorkie live a long, healthy, active life.

Your veterinarian will probably recommend that your Yorkie be spayed or neutered. He or she will also emphasize the importance of regular exercise. Both of these things are important to continued good health. But play is important, too, for both you and your Yorkie, and we'll talk about why.

Watch Out!

Make sure you read the breeder's, rescue group's, or shelter's contract carefully. Many require action of some kind should the newly adopted puppy or dog have a health problem. Make sure you know what to do.

A Partner in Your Yorkie's Health

A veterinarian you trust will be a great help to you in maintaining your Yorkie's good health. Even long-time dog owners can have questions about canine health, and your veterinarian is the person to ask. Your neighbor, friend, or relative may offer help, but they may also give you incorrect or incomplete information.

 Watch Out!

Don't wait until there's an emergency to find a veterinarian. Do your research before you need help. Yellow page ads are fine and coupons in the mail are okay, but keep in mind anyone can place an ad. However, people who have done business with veterinarians can tell you about firsthand experiences.

You can find veterinarians in your area in several different ways, but the most reliable is usually by personal referrals. If you ask several dog owners which veterinarian they recommend, and one name keeps popping up, well, he or she would probably be a good choice.

Make an Appointment

When you have a few referrals to some veterinarians, call and make an appointment to meet with each one. They may or may not ask for you to pay for their time, but if they do, please remember their time is their money! When you meet with them, ask a few questions:

- What are their business hours?

- What is the business telephone number?

- What are their payment procedures? Do they have any financing for emergencies or do they accept credit cards? Which ones?

≈ Are the veterinarians familiar with health problems Yorkies might face?

After you decide which veterinarian you feel most comfortable with, set up a client chart with him. Your veterinarian will want to examine your Yorkie within the first couple of days after you bring the dog home. Most breeders, rescue groups, and shelters request (and some require) that the dog be examined soon after purchase or adoption. This examination can assure you of the dog's good health or pinpoint any potential health problems. If your dog came with a health guarantee, this visit is a necessary part of the agreement.

Bet You Didn't Know

In the text, I refer to the veterinarian as a "he" for simplicity's sake—it's awkward to write or read "he or she." However, by doing so, I mean no disrespect to female veterinarians; they have my highest respect. In fact, more women are attending vet schools today than men!

During the exam, the vet will look the Yorkie over carefully, looking at his eyes, ears, teeth, skin, hair coat, and genitals. He will look at the outside of the Yorkie for outward problems and then will begin examining the Yorkie with his hands. He will feel for anything that is out of the ordinary or feels like a potential problem. He will watch the Yorkie as he moves his hands over the Yorkie's body to see if the Yorkie tenses or winces when touched. This could signal soreness from rough play, an injury, or an illness.

Your vet may also be looking for congenital problems. If the Yorkie has untreatable or potentially expensive health problems, or is genetically unhealthy, you have the right (if you so desire) to return the Yorkie to the breeder. If the Yorkie has a problem and

Bet You Didn't Know

Some people seem to resent the money spent at the veterinarian's office. However, your vet's goal is to keep your Yorkie healthy, and any money spent in preventative medicine is money well spent!

you decide to keep him anyway, the breeder should be willing to give you a full or partial refund.

If you adopted your Yorkie from a rescue group or a shelter, there will probably be no health guarantee. However, if there are drastic health problems, you may decide to return the dog before you are too emotionally attached to him. If you decide to keep this Yorkie, even with health problems, knowing about those health problems right away can help you deal with them or prepare for them.

Recognizing Problems

Your Yorkie should visit the veterinarian's office at least once per year even if he seems perfectly healthy to you. If your vet is giving vaccinations on an annual basis, this is the time to give those shots. However, if your vet is giving vaccinations on a different schedule, your Yorkie should still see the vet once per year. During these annual visits, your vet can evaluate your dog's health, see any changes from the previous year's visit, and hopefully catch any problems before they become a bigger problem.

However, because you see your dog every day, you are the best person to catch problems early. Pay attention to anything that changes in your dog's actions. For example, a lack of appetite may simply mean your dog is hot, and he may eat later in the evening when the weather is cooler, but a lack of appetite over several meals may signal something worse.

Call your veterinarian if you notice any of these potential problems:

- A temperature of lower than 100 degrees or higher than 102.5.
- Diarrhea that lasts more than one day, or that contains a significant amount of mucus or has blood in it.
- Vomiting that continues more than a couple hours.
- Loss of appetite for more than two meals.
- Distended abdomen and obvious tenderness.

- Fainting, collapse, or seizures.

- Potential allergic reactions, including swelling, hives, or rashes, especially around the face.

- Respiratory distress, including coughing that won't stop, trouble breathing, or a suspected obstruction.

- Potential poisonings, especially antifreeze, rodent poisons, snail poisons, insecticides, or herbicides.

- Cuts or wounds that gape open or don't stop bleeding with direct pressure.

- Suspected snake bites, bites from other wild animals, spiders, cats, and even other dogs.

- A leg that is held up, with no weight put on it, and is obviously hurt.

- Eye injuries—they are almost always emergencies.

- Housetraining accidents that are not normal behavior.

- Changes in behavior (crying and whining, growling, grumpiness) that have not been caused by known influences (such as changes in routine or guests in the house).

Some things are not quite as obvious but could still signal trouble. Call your veterinarian for advice if you see any of the following:

- Your Yorkie is hiding and won't come out.

- Your Yorkie is panting when the weather and his activity levels don't warrant it.

- Your Yorkie is restless for no apparent reason.

- Your Yorkie refuses to participate in normal activities.

Watch Out!
Never ignore any of these warning signs in the hope that they may go away. Waiting could be dangerous for your Yorkie.

Tell Your Vet Everything

When you call your veterinarian with a suspected problem, tell him everything. Don't assume that something may be too trivial or is unimportant. Instead, tell him everything you can possibly think of and let him worry about the significance of it. That's where his knowledge and experience come in.

In return, your vet will ask you some questions. Expect, at the minimum, these questions:

- What is the specific problem or the symptom that causes you to think there is a problem?
- What made you notice it?
- What are all the symptoms or the behaviors that are out of the ordinary?
- What is your dog's rectal temperature?
- Has he eaten? When and how much?
- Is there any vomiting? If so, what was vomited up?
- Is there diarrhea? When and how often? What does it look like? Is there mucus or blood in the feces?
- Has the dog been in contact with anything out of the ordinary? Did he get into the trash? Or have you been traveling?
- How long has this been going on?

Listen to Your Vet

When your veterinarian is talking to you, listen. Listen carefully and take notes if you want. Make sure you know what to do with your Yorkie. If he has prescribed medication, find out how much medication you should give and when. Make sure you know when the vet wants to see your dog again. Get all the information so that you can care for your dog as best you can.

Spaying and Neutering Are Important!

Most female Yorkies should be spayed and males neutered. The only Yorkies who should be bred are those who are the best in physical conformation, temperament, and genetic health. By breeding only the best of the breed, you are helping to make sure that future puppies are even healthier than those of today, with fewer genetic defects and with good, sound temperaments.

Just because a particular Yorkie is a wonderful pet and well loved by all who live with him or her, it doesn't make that dog a good candidate for breeding. A well-loved pet may not be of correct physical conformation as per the breed standard and may carry unknown genetic defects.

Breeding Dogs Isn't Easy

Breeding is a big job. To do it correctly, research must be conducted into the ancestors of the male and female being considered for breeding. Were the ancestors of these two dogs of correct physical conformation? Did any of their offspring produce any puppies with problems, emotionally or physically? Did any of their offspring have health problems? Did they live long, healthy lives?

Besides the research involved, the breeding process itself can be stressful. Sometimes the male will need help and often the female will not want to cooperate. Could you help if your dog doesn't want to be involved? It's not easy.

There can also be problems during pregnancy or before, during, and after birth. Tiny female Yorkies often need help during delivery. The tiny puppies also occasionally need help to thrive. Are you ready to bottle raise a litter if the mother doesn't have any milk, or worse yet, just decides she wants nothing to do with the puppies? It happens!

Then what happens when those puppies need homes? If your dog is simply a well-loved pet, with no championship, obedience, or agility titles to attest to her abilities, will anyone want your puppies? Don't count on that neighbor or friend who said they wanted one when your dog was a puppy; those people disappear quickly when puppies are actually available.

Unfortunately, many people breed their dogs, or allow their dogs to be bred, without knowing the realities of responsible dog breeding. The end result is hundreds of thousands of dogs born only to be killed in shelters. And yes, even Yorkies have been euthanized in shelters. As I write this today, there is a Yorkshire Terrier in each of the three local shelters within driving distance of my home. They will, unfortunately, remain there because the rescue groups are full and cannot take in any more. There are too many people breeding Yorkies and too few homes available.

Bet You Didn't Know

Every dog who is given up as unwanted costs taxpayers money.

Mandatory Spay and Neuter Laws

The thousands upon thousands of dogs who have ended up in shelters across the country cost taxpayers money; not just to feed and house them, but also the people to staff the shelters and run animal control. When these dogs are added to the dogs causing problems in communities, especially dog bite situations, dogs become more of a problem than a benefit. Because of this, many cities and communities across the United States are trying to regulate dog breeding. Many have instituted fines or costly licenses to discourage dog breeding.

A healthy Yorkie can live for 15 to 16 years.

These measures may hamper or discourage the reputable, responsible breeder because that person is more apt to pay attention to animal laws in the community and abide by them. Unfortunately, these laws won't do anything to control indiscriminate, accidental breedings or breeding by backyard breeders who have no idea what the local laws are. Many communities have instituted mandatory spay and neuter laws and they just don't work.

Voluntary Spaying and Neutering

What does work is education. When pet owners understand what spaying a female dog does and does not do; when owners understand what neutering a male dog does and does not do; and when pet owners understand the scope of the pet overpopulation problem; they are far more likely to spay and neuter their pet dogs.

Traditionally, dogs have been spayed or neutered at about six months of age. However, many humane societies—in an effort to

Yorkie Smarts

A female who has been spayed will no longer go through her two to three times per year "season." She will no longer spot on the floors and male dogs will no longer come "calling."

curtail breeding—have been spaying and neutering very young puppies, some as young as eight weeks of age.

What Happens?

Spaying a female dog consists of a surgical ovariohysterectomy. The ovaries and uterus are removed through an incision in the abdomen. Your veterinarian will tell you to keep her quiet for a few days so she doesn't hurt herself, but most dogs show very few ill effects from the surgery. Most bounce back very quickly.

Yorkie Smarts

Have you heard that a spayed or neutered dog will get fat? That's a myth. Dogs get fat when they are given too much food and not enough exercise!

Male dogs are neutered (castrated), which consists of removing the testicles through an incision just in front of the scrotum. Again, your vet will tell you to keep him quiet for a few days. Most male puppies have very little pain afterward, usually acting as if nothing has happened.

Other Benefits

Spaying or neutering your Yorkie has a number of health and behavioral benefits besides simply stopping reproduction.

For females, spaying …

🦴 Decreases the incidence of mammary gland cancer.

🦴 Protects against cancers of the reproductive system.

🦴 Decreases the incidence of female aggression.

For males, neutering …

🦴 Decreases male sexual behaviors, including leg-lifting, marking, roaming, and fighting.

🦴 Decreases the urge to escape from the yard.

🦴 Protects him from testicular cancer.

Taking Care of Your Yorkie

Most of this book is focused on helping you care for your Yorkie in one way or another, so having a section titled "Taking Care of Your Yorkie" may seem superfluous. However, let's take a look at some specific things that can help you care for your Yorkie as best you can. When you take reasonable care, and do so consciously, you are better equipped to keep your Yorkie as safe and healthy as possible.

Maintain Safety

Hopefully you puppy-proofed your house and yard before you brought home your Yorkie—as we discussed in Chapter 2—but have you kept it that way? It's very easy to forget to put things away, and some car repair chemicals, pool supplies, or fertilizer for the backyard could kill your Yorkie should he decide to get into them. It's important to maintain puppy-proofing—that level of safety that we discussed.

Yorkies are incredibly curious and will stick their noses into places where they have no right to be. They are this way because they were rodent hunters, and rodents hide in those places. Unfortunately, it can also get them into trouble. Look at life from your Yorkie's point of view. He is tiny, very low to the ground, and his viewpoint is very different from yours.

Yorkies are also incredibly athletic and can easily learn to climb obstacles. It only takes one exploration trip for a Yorkie to learn that if he climbs up on a hassock, he can then get on a chair, and from the back of the chair he can reach the birdcage. Using similar techniques, he can access cupboards or shelves that you probably thought were safe.

Being overly protective in this regard is not bad and, in fact, could save your dog's life.

Common Sense

Common sense also plays a big part in keeping your Yorkie safe. Don't let him explore the garage if it's not safe. Put childproof locks on cupboard doors. Don't let him off his leash outside a fenced-in yard until he's grown up and very well trained and, even then, don't let him off-leash near a street.

Common sense and reasonable care will go a long way toward keeping your Yorkie safe.

Get Out and Have Some Fun!

Yorkies are usually added to a family as a companion dog; most often a lap dog. They are usually companion dogs for adults, as other breeds make better companions for kids. What many people forget, though, is that Yorkies were not bred (originally) as lap dogs. Yorkies may be tiny and incredibly cute, but they are still terriers with an urge to do stuff, instincts to hunt, and a lot of natural athletic abilities.

> **Watch Out!**
>
> Begin any exercise program slowly. Just as with people, Yorkies can get sore muscles from doing new or strenuous activities.

Yorkies are active dogs. They need to run and jump, to explore safe places, and smell new smells. Yorkies need activities that will keep their mind active and their body healthy. A Yorkie who lives his life on a lap without exercise, playtime, and mental stimulation will not thrive. He will get fat, lose muscle tone, and his mind will get dull. How sad!

Exercise Ideas

One of the benefits of a tiny dog—as compared to larger breeds—is that exercise is much easier. It's tough to exercise a Great Dane in a small house, but very easy to exercise a Yorkie!

Experts have studied play and say that it's good for our mental and physical health, as well as for our social skills. The same applies to your Yorkie!

Exercise ideas for inside the house:

- Play retrieving games by throwing a ball or toy across the room or down the hall.

- Extend your foot or leg as you are sitting and teach your Yorkie to jump over it.

- Use some of your furniture as agility equipment. Have your Yorkie jump up on to the hassock, crawl under the coffee table, and dash the length of the sofa.

Exercise ideas for the backyard:

- Play retrieving games, throwing a ball or toy across the yard.

- Call him to come between two people, taking turns, and encouraging him to run as

Bet You Didn't Know

It's important to remember that when you are simply walking, your Yorkie is running. Try to moderate your pace so he can keep up without getting exhausted.

fast as he can back and forth a few times. Stop before he gets too tired or loses interest.

Exercise ideas outside:

- Go for walks in different places.
- Go for a hike in a local woods or meadow.
- Go for a jog at the local park.

It's Playtime!

Play is important to all sentient creatures, both young and old. Researchers have been telling us for years that play in the young is preparation for adulthood, but recent research has shown it's important for other reasons, too. Playtime helps animals bond with other members of their group. It builds relationships and makes them stronger. When two beings (human or other animals) play together, they feel a kinship for each other and seem to be more likely to support one another.

Play between a dog and owner is very much the same. If you and your dog don't play together, the relationship lacks something that is hard to describe. The sense of fun and of pleasure isn't there; the sense of companionship isn't the same. However, when you play with your dog, the two of you can relax, laugh, enjoy each other's company, and simply have fun.

Playtime can be a part of exercise, especially if you play physical games such as retrieving games. But playtime can also be separate from exercise. Playtime also doesn't have to be anything formal; you don't have to do anything specific. Just sit on the floor, roll your Yorkie over, and rub his tummy as you talk silly to him. Let him bounce up and run circles around you as you pat the floor and threaten to catch him. Play can be, and at times certainly should be, silly.

Yorkie Smarts

Most dog trainers, myself included, usually tell dog owners not to wrestle and play tug of war with their dogs because it teaches the dog to use his strength against you. However, Yorkies are so small and you are so much bigger, it's usually not a problem. Go ahead and play!

That Special Bond

People get dogs for a variety of reasons. Some may want a protector and guardian, and feel safer with a dog's ears and instincts guarding them. Some people want a jogging companion and a playmate. Many people know that a dog is a social magnet! What dog owners know, though, even if only subconsciously, is that we feel more complete when we share our life with a dog (or two or three).

The bond that a dog and owner feel is one that happens with no other pets or animals. I have cats and love them very much, but I don't have the bond with them that I do with my dogs. Horse owners say the same thing; their horses are special, but the relationship isn't quite the same.

When a dog and owner have that bond, they feel responsible for each other. They watch and look out for each other. There is affection and love, but there is also respect.

That bond develops through time spent together. Exercise, playtime and laughter, companionship, and quiet times all work toward building that bond. There will not be a certain instant when you will notice, "Hey, we're bonded!" No, it develops more gradually than that. You'll know you've bonded with your dog when you find that you want to spend time with him; when he's not by your side you miss him. You know you're bonded when you worry when he's got a burr in his paw, or when he doesn't want to eat dinner. When you can't imagine life without him—you're bonded!

The Least You Need to Know

- Work with your veterinarian to keep your Yorkie healthy.

- Spaying and neutering will help avoid unwanted puppies, and offers other health and behavioral benefits.

- Common sense and reasonable care will help keep your Yorkie safe.

- Exercise and playtime are important for your Yorkie's continued good health and to help cement the bond between you both.

Chapter 17

Health Problems to Watch Out For

In This Chapter

- Making sense of health problems
- Remembering that small dogs have special problems
- Vaccinating against dangerous diseases
- Fighting fleas, ticks, and other bugs

This chapter covers some of the less appealing aspects of dog ownership. After all, no one wants to know that their beloved Yorkie might have a serious health problem. However, knowledge is a good thing, and we'll just hope you never need to use it!

This chapter discusses some of the health problems Yorkies can face, including the special problems tiny dogs can have. We'll also talk about those nasty parasites all dogs can pick up and what you can do about them.

Inherited Health Problems and Birth Defects

Genetic health problems are inherited from the puppy's ancestors. Either the mother or father had the gene causing the problem, or both had the genes, or one or both were carriers of the gene. Research has been ongoing and will probably continue for many years as to how genetic diseases are passed, but many questions remain to be answered.

> **Dog Talk**
>
> **Genetic health problems** are inherited. **Congenital health threats** are present at birth but may or may not be inherited.

Congenital health threats (often called birth defects) are present at birth but may or may not be hereditary. Identifying which health problems are genetic or congenital is also the subject of much study.

The Nervous System

Although epilepsy and other seizure disorders are not common in Yorkies, they are not unheard of. Seizures may be as mild as a "freezing," where the dog doesn't or can't move, to a grand mal seizure with strong convulsions. Experts now believe that most seizure disorders are inherited, although this has yet to be proven. Seizures can also be caused by trauma to the head, by exposure to toxins, or even by other diseases.

If your Yorkie has a seizure, make him comfortable and don't allow him to hurt himself, but don't try to stop the seizure. After the seizure, he'll be groggy and disorientated for a little while. Take him to the veterinarian's office as soon as possible after the seizure; blood tests can sometimes pinpoint the cause of the seizure.

The Internal Organs

Some Yorkies have been found to have a developmental defect involving the blood supply and the liver. During fetal development, blood bypasses the liver. However, shortly after birth, this bypass should close, allowing the blood to go through the liver so that the liver can remove toxins and wastes from the blood. When the bypass does not close, the blood is not cleansed and gradually the dog sickens. This condition, called portosystemic liver shunt, or portacaval shunt, can sometimes be corrected with surgery. It usually shows up in fairly young dogs—younger than six months of age. Puppies with this condition do not thrive, do not gain weight, and sometimes have seizures.

Yorkies have also been known to have Cushing's disease, also known as hyperadrenocorticism. In this disease, the adrenal glands produce excess hormones, causing many different symptoms and problems including poor muscle tone, nervous system disorders, hair loss, excess thirst and urination, and high blood pressure. The condition tends to show up in older dogs. If you notice any of these symptoms, talk to your vet immediately.

The Eyes

Yorkies have fewer problems with their eyes than many other breeds. Older dogs may develop cataracts, although this is more of an aging problem than a congenital or genetic problem. Occasionally some Yorkies have dry eyes, a problem that is usually related to the tear glands and ducts. Dry eyes require veterinary care, so if your Yorkie rubs his eyes a lot, blinks, squints, or keeps his eyes closed, see your veterinarian right away. If the eyes are not treated immediately, the corneas can become scarred, causing permanent damage.

The Skin

Yorkies can be allergic to many things, including grass, pollen, dust mites, and flea bites. The skin usually appears red, sometimes with bug bites apparent, but not always. Your Yorkie will also scratch a lot and chew on himself. Some dogs itch so badly they mutilate themselves, so this is not something to ignore. Dogs suffering with skin allergies are miserable. See your vet right away so they can stop the allergic reaction; then you need to try and figure out what's causing the problem, and your vet can guide you through that process.

The Skeletal System

The most common skeletal problem seen in the breed is luxated patellas. In this disorder, the kneecap (patella) is not held in place properly, causing the dog to hop and skip until it moves back into place. The extent of the disorder may range from very mild—when the dog just skips once in a while—to more severe—with the dog holding a leg up and crying in pain. Depending on the extent of the problem, your vet may recommend corrective surgery.

Legg-Calve-Perthes Disease is also seen in Yorkies. In this disease, a poor blood supply to the head of the femur (thighbone) causes the bone to deteriorate. First symptoms appear in late puppyhood and may show up simply as limping. As the disease progresses, symptoms worsen until no weight is put on the leg at all. Surgery is usually recommended.

Bet You Didn't Know

The Orthopedic Foundation for Animals (OFA) and PennHIP maintain lists of dogs who have been x-rayed for hip and elbow dysplasia. Breeders can then research the lists and eliminate from their breeding plan any dog who has dysplasia or has produced dogs with questionable elbows and/or hips.

Hip dysplasia is a deformity of the hip joint. The dog may show lameness and may not want to move. Although this is more common in larger breeds, it is, unfortunately, being seen in more and more small dogs and has been found in Yorkies. Although surgery is sometimes an option, with tiny dogs such as Yorkies, sometimes veterinary management is recommended rather than surgery. Talk to your vet about options.

Elbow dysplasia is a deformity of the elbow, much like hip dysplasia, and will show up as lameness and a lack of desire to move. This is not common in Yorkies but has been seen in the breed.

Small Dogs Have Special Problems

Their size makes small dogs susceptible to some special problems. Obviously, small dogs are more fragile, and if stepped on or inadvertently kicked, may suffer from broken bones or internal injuries. Many tiny Yorkies have been hurt when they were asleep on a chair or sofa and someone accidentally sat on them! Accidents will happen, unfortunately, but take care to prevent as many as possible.

Watch Out!

Get into the habit of looking for your Yorkie. Look where you step and look before you sit down.

Many toy breeds, including Yorkies, suffer from hypoglycemia (low blood sugar). In dogs with hypoglycemia, when blood sugar levels drop too far, the dogs will become weak, drowsy, and disoriented, and if it progresses the dog can have a seizure or go into a coma. This is most common in puppies, and many will grow out of it. It is most commonly seen in the very tiny Yorkies (less than 4 to 5 pounds when full grown). These dogs should eat two or three meals per day, and the condition requires veterinary assistance and management.

It is not uncommon to hear tiny dogs, including Yorkies, coughing. Sometimes the cough is caused by the dog pulling on the leash. When the leash puts pressure on the trachea, the trachea may give, bend, or even partially collapse, causing the dog to cough or even gasp for air. If the dog has a weak trachea, even hard breathing during play or exercise could cause a partial trachea collapse, again causing coughing or gasping. If this happens, the veterinarian should be consulted for possible treatments. Training can teach the Yorkie not to pull on the leash.

Dangerous Canine Diseases

Unfortunately, there are many diseases that are very dangerous to dogs. Some, as with rabies, are almost always fatal, while others, such as coronavirus, will just make the dog sick.

Most of these diseases have a vaccination that can help protect the dog from getting the disease. However, because over-vaccinating the dog can be just as threatening to the dog's health as not vaccinating him, deciding which vaccines to give should be decided after discussing your options with your veterinarian. Vaccines will be discussed in the next section.

Rabies

The rabies virus is carried by infected wildlife and is highly contagious. It is transmitted in the saliva, either through a break in the skin or by a bite. It is always fatal.

> **Watch Out!**
> Never allow your Yorkie to play with a wild animal, especially one that's acting strangely. Bats, skunks, and raccoons have been known to carry rabies.

Distemper

This is a contagious viral disease. Dogs with distemper have a fever, are weak and depressed, have a discharge from the eyes and nose, cough, vomit, and have diarrhea. Many will show neurological symptoms, including staggering and lack of coordination. The virus is passed through the saliva, urine, and feces. Most infected dogs die.

Parvovirus

Commonly called parvo, parvovirus is a terrible killer of puppies. It attacks the inner lining of the intestines, causing bloody diarrhea. This diarrhea has a very distinctive smell that veterinarians and breeders who have dealt with the disease quickly learn to recognize.

In young puppies, the disease also attacks the heart, causing death, often with no other symptoms. The virus replicates very quickly, and dehydration can lead to shock and death within a matter of hours.

Infectious Canine Hepatitis

Infectious canine hepatitis is another highly contagious viral disease. It primarily attacks the liver but can also damage the kidneys. It is not related to the human forms of hepatitis. The virus is spread through the saliva, mucus, urine, and feces. Initial symptoms include depression, vomiting, abdominal pain, fever, and jaundice. Mild cases can be treated, but the mortality rate is very high.

Coronavirus

Coronavirus is rarely fatal for adult dogs but can be very dangerous for puppies. Symptoms include vomiting and loose, watery diarrhea. The virus is shed in the stools. Dehydration from the diarrhea and vomiting is the primary danger for puppies.

Leptospirosis

Leptospirosis is caused by bacteria, not a virus, and is passed in the urine. The bacteria attack the kidneys, causing kidney failure. Symptoms include fever, loss of appetite, possibly diarrhea, and jaundice. Antibiotics can sometimes treat the disease, but some dogs die, primarily due to the tremendous damage the bacteria cause.

The vaccinations can usually prevent the disease, although leptospirosis can appear in different forms (serovars) and the vaccine may not protect against all forms. Care must be taken to not spread this highly contagious disease; it can spread to people and other dogs.

Kennel Cough

Tracheobronchitis, adenovirus, and parainfluenza are a few of the diseases commonly referred to as kennel cough or canine cough. All

Bet You Didn't Know ?

Kennel Cough got its name because when one dog in a kennel situation begins coughing, it usually spreads throughout the kennel.

three of these cause significant coughing, sometimes with a fever, sometimes without. Most healthy adult dogs can recuperate from these without veterinary care; however, young puppies and older dogs need careful monitoring, as a secondary respiratory infection can occur. In some cases, pneumonia develops.

Vaccinations usually prevent these diseases; however, viruses can and do mutate and often well-vaccinated dogs will still come down with some form of kennel cough. Kennel cough can be best compared to a human cold; we don't know exactly what causes either of them and, in fact, the causes may be numerous.

Vaccinations

A puppy from a breeder or a dog from a shelter or rescue has probably already received some vaccinations. If you have the vaccination records (try to get them if you don't), bring them with you to the vet's office. Your veterinarian will set up a vaccination schedule depending on the vaccinations already given.

Dog Talk

Vaccines are either modified live or killed vaccines. Modified live vaccines are considered more effective but do carry a small risk of transmitting disease.

Vaccinations work by giving the dog an inactive form of the disease so the dog can develop the right antibodies (disease-fighting cells) without the threat of getting sick. Most vaccines stimulate the body to produce antibodies for a period of time. Booster shots are then given to continue the protection.

Vaccinations are most often given for the following diseases:

Rabies	Coronavirus
Distemper	Adenovirus
Parvovirus	Parainfluenza
Hepatitis	Bordatella
Leptospirosis	Lyme disease

Which Vaccines?

Your veterinarian will recommend a vaccination schedule depending on where you live and which diseases are seen in your area. For example, if coronavirus isn't a problem in your region, your vet may not feel it's important to give your dog that vaccine. However, if you will be traveling to an area where coronavirus is common, you should mention that to your vet.

Potential Problems

Modern vaccines have saved millions of dogs' lives, but that doesn't mean vaccines are risk-free. Unfortunately, vaccinations do have some risks associated with them.

The most common side effect of a vaccination is a small, hard lump that forms at the injection site a few days after the injection. This is called a sterile abscess and needs no treatment; it will go away on its own.

Allergic reactions may also occur after a vaccination. Mild reactions may include shivering, a low-grade fever, or redness at the injection site. Some allergic reactions can be quite serious, however, including anaphylactic shock. Anaphylactic shock can be life threatening and always requires immediate veterinary

Yorkie Smarts

You are responsible for your Yorkie's health and care, so don't hesitate to ask as many questions of your veterinarian as you wish. He shouldn't take offense to your questions. Just ask them nicely, of course!

care. Because of the dangers of an allergic reaction, always remain at the vet's office for at least 30 minutes after your dog has received a vaccination—even if you just sit in the waiting room—to make sure your dog isn't going to have a reaction.

Too Many Vaccinations?

Recent research has begun to question the wisdom of giving vaccination boosters every year, as has been the common practice. Many veterinarians, breeders, dog owners, and researchers are coming to believe that too many vaccinations—either at the same time or too close together—may be damaging dogs' immune systems.

Some veterinarians are now giving booster vaccinations every 18 months instead of every 12 months; and some veterinary schools are recommending that many boosters can be safely given every 36 months instead of 12!

Talk to your vet about the vaccination schedule he proposes. How close together is he scheduling shots? How many doses does he give at one time? Is he concerned about the frequency of booster shots? Make sure you understand what he's giving your dog, how much, and why before you okay the vaccination schedule.

> **Watch Out!**
>
> The dangers associated with vaccines don't mean you shouldn't have your dog vaccinated at all; the dangers caused by the diseases themselves are much, much greater!

Only the Healthy!

Your Yorkie should be vaccinated only when he is healthy. If he's not feeling well, he's at increased risk of getting sick from the vaccination itself, or his immune system may not respond well to the vaccination. In addition, the stress of the vaccination may make his original illness worse, depending, of course, on what the original illness is.

Fleas, Ticks, and Other Bugs!

External parasites—fleas, ticks, and mites—are insects that are uniquely suited to pester your dog. Fleas, ticks, and mites have a long history of destruction behind them, too. Fleas have been blamed for innumerable plagues throughout history, including the bubonic plague that decimated Europe many years ago. Today these are still pests and can still threaten your dog's comfort and health, although we have a much better arsenal at our fingertips to combat them.

Fleas

A flea is a small, slightly crescent-shaped, six-legged insect with a big abdomen and a small head. It's a tremendous jumper and is flat sided, so it can slip through hair with ease. When caught, it will pop under (or between) your fingernails like a tiny balloon. If that sounds gross, you obviously haven't dealt with too many fleas! Fleas cause dogs so much torment, it can be very satisfying to pop the little pests!

Fleas live by biting your dog, taking a drop or two of blood each time they bite. A heavy infestation can actually cause anemia from the blood-loss in Yorkies. Many dogs are so allergic to flea bites, the poor dogs will scratch, dig, and chew themselves raw. An allergic dog could end up with flea bite dermatitis or open sores, which could then develop into secondary infections.

> **Bet You Didn't Know**
>
> To check for fleas, place your Yorkie on a solid-colored sheet. Brush his coat thoroughly then let him up. If you see salt and pepper type residue, your dog has fleas. The residue is fecal matter (the "pepper") and eggs (the "salt").

Fleas are also the intermediate host for tapeworms, which will be discussed later in this chapter. If your dog has fleas and, during chewing, swallows a tapeworm-infected flea, the dog can then become infested with tapeworms. Fleas can also carry diseases, including bubonic plague. Obviously, then, these pests are more than simply annoying to you and your dog; they are also a very real health threat.

Fortunately, in the past few years several products have been introduced to make flea control easier and safer. In past years, insecticides and pesticides were the only available products, and you had to use those with caution. If you weren't careful, you could easily end up poisoning yourself and your dog before you killed off all the fleas.

Some new options include ...

- **Systemic topical treatments.** These products are applied to the skin, usually between the shoulder blades, and the product is absorbed into the dog's system. Depending on the product, the flea is killed when it bites the dog or its reproductive cycle is disrupted.

- **Systemic products.** Your dog swallows a pill, which transmits a chemical throughout the body. When the flea bites the dog, it picks up this chemical. The chemical prevents the flea's eggs from developing and hence, the insect population dies off.

- **Insect growth regulators (IGRs).** These products stop the immature flea from developing or maturing, thus preventing it from reproducing.

To control fleas you must hit them in three ways: on the dog, in your house, and in your yard. Leave out any one of the three, and your control efforts will fail. If you have found fleas on your dog, then you can be sure that you have them in the house and in the yard, because the fleas are on your dog only to feed; they do not live on the dog. They live in your house and yard!

Watch Out!

Always read the directions on all flea control products. Make sure you use them correctly to keep your dog and your family safe.

Some control methods might include the following:

- **In the yard.** Use a spray designed for outside use that contains an IGR. Repeat as recommended.

- **In the house.** Use a spray for inside use with an IGR. If your house is infested, use a spray with a quick kill ingredient as well as an IGR. Use according to directions.

- **On the dog.** Use a systemic product such as Program or Sentinel. Do not use insecticides or flea collars in addition to the systemic product unless the label on both products specifies that it is safe to do so.

Ticks

Ticks are eight-legged, oblong insects with a head that embeds into the skin. Ticks feed on the host's blood and, when engorged, will drop off. Ticks, as with fleas, are carriers of human and canine diseases. In the United States, they carry Rocky Mountain Spotted Fever and Lyme disease, as well as other diseases. Rocky Mountain Spotted Fever is an acutely infectious disease that is characterized by muscular pains, high fevers, and skin eruptions. Lyme disease, which affects dogs as well as people, causes a lingering fever and joint pain (sometimes quite severe) and can also cause neurological problems.

Yorkie Smarts

Ask your veterinarian if Lyme disease is a problem in your area. If so, find out if he recommends giving the Lyme disease vaccination.

Although some flea products are partially effective on ticks, they are rarely totally effective at killing or keeping ticks off your dog. During tick season (spring and summer) you will have to examine your dog daily and remove each and every tick. Check your dog all over, but pay especially close attention to ticks' favorite spots: behind or in the ears, in the armpit area of the front legs, and around the neck.

Never remove a tick with your bare fingers. Use tweezers or wear rubber gloves. Grab down close to the skin and pull gently but firmly, with a slow twisting motion so that the head comes out with the body of the tick. If you just pull the tick straight out, the head could remain in the skin, potentially causing an infection or abscess.

Don't flush the tick; it will survive its trip downstream and live to bite again or worse yet, reproduce! Instead burn it to kill it. Put a little antibiotic ointment on the wound where the tick was embedded.

Mange Mites

Mange is usually associated with stray dogs who have no one to care for them. This isn't necessarily so. Many well-loved dogs have come down with mange one way or another.

Mange is caused by mites—tiny microscopic pests—that live on the dog. Your veterinarian will do a skin scraping to look at under the microscope to see if mites are present. Mange comes in two varieties:

- **Sarcoptic mange** is contagious to people and other pets. Its primary symptoms include red welts, and the dog will be scratching continuously. Sarcoptic mange usually responds well to treatment.

- **Demodectic mange** is not considered contagious and shows up with bald patches, usually first on the dog's face, and there may not be any scratching or itching. Demodectic mange often appears in young dogs and will clear up with treatment. However, in older dogs, treatment can be long and drawn out and is sometimes not effective at all.

Watch Out!

Suspected mange mite infestations should always be seen by a veterinarian for diagnosis and treatment.

Ringworm

Ringworm isn't really a worm at all, but instead is a very contagious fungus that infests the skin and causes ring-shaped (round), scaly, itchy spots. These round spots are the trademark identification of ringworm. It is spread by contact; perhaps from another dog, a cat, or even a wild animal.

Ringworm usually responds well to treatment, but care must be taken to follow the treatment plan according to directions as set up by your veterinarian because this is very, very contagious to people and other pets.

Ickk! Bugs Inside!

Internal parasites are just as disgusting as external parasites but can be more threatening to your dog's health because they are not as easily seen. You will see fleas on your dog, for example, but your dog could have internal parasites for quite a while before you notice any signs of poor health.

Most internal parasites can be detected by taking a small piece of your dog's stool to the veterinarian's office. The stool will be prepared and then examined under a microscope. Parasites, the eggs, or larvae can then be detected, and your vet can prescribe appropriate treatment. After treatment, your vet will ask you to bring in another stool sample—usually in two to three weeks—to make sure the treatment was effective. Parasites that dogs are susceptible to include the following:

- **Heartworms.** Heartworms live in the upper heart and greater pulmonary arteries, damaging the blood vessel walls. Poor circulation results, which in turn damages other body functions. Eventually, the heart fails and the dog dies. The adult worms produce thousands of tiny worms known as microfilaria. These circulate throughout the bloodstream until they are picked up by mosquitoes; the intermediate host. The microfilaria continue to develop in the mosquito, then, when they're ready, they can be transferred to another dog when that mosquito bites it. Preventive medications are available, easy to administer, and very effective. Talk to your veterinarian about heartworm preventatives and whether heartworm has been found in your area. If heartworm is present, your vet will recommend a blood test to make sure your Yorkie has not already been infected. If the blood sample comes back okay, your vet will prescribe a preventative medication.

Watch Out!

Roundworm eggs can be picked up via feces—your Yorkie should be discouraged from sniffing other dogs' feces.

- **Roundworms.** These long, white worms are fairly common in puppies, although they can also be found in adult dogs and humans, as well as other animals. A dog with roundworms will not thrive and will appear thin, with a dull coat and a pot belly. Often you will see worms in the stool or vomit. Roundworms can be detected by your veterinarian through a fecal analysis. Good sanitation is important to prevent an infestation; feces should be picked up and disposed of daily.

- **Hookworms.** Hookworms live in the small intestine where they attach to the intestinal wall and suck blood. When they detach and move to a new location, the old wound continues to bleed for a period of time, causing bloody diarrhea, which is often a symptom of a hookworm infestation. Hookworm eggs are passed through the feces and are picked up from the stools, as with roundworms. The eggs can be detected in a fecal analysis. Treatment often needs to be repeated two or more times before finally ridding the dog of the parasites. Good sanitation is necessary to prevent a re-infestation. Hookworms can also be spread to people.

- **Tapeworms.** Tapeworms live in the intestinal tract and attach to the wall to absorb nutrients. They grow by creating new segments. Usually the first sign of an infestation are small rice-like segments found around the dog's rectum or in his stool. Tapeworms are acquired when the dog eats an infected flea, the intermediate host, or catches and eats rodents such as mice, which can be hosts. Your vet can prescribe treatment but a good flea control program is the best way to prevent future tapeworm infestations.

Watch Out!

If your dog has had whipworms, talk to your vet about treating your yard, because whipworm eggs can live in the soil for years.

🦴 **Whipworms.** Whipworms live in the large intestine, where they feed on blood. The eggs are passed in the feces and can live in the soil for a long time—years, even. A dog who eats the fresh spring grass or buries his bone in the infected soil can pick up eggs. Heavy infestations can cause diarrhea, and the dog will appear thin and anemic, with a poor coat. Whipworms are not as easily detected through fecal analysis as other worms, as they don't shed eggs in the stool as frequently as do roundworms and hookworms. Several stool samples may need to be checked to be certain. If caught early, your vet can prescribe treatment but heavy infestations can be fatal.

🦴 **Giardiasis.** The parasitic protozoa giardia is common in wild animals. If you and your dog go camping or hiking and take a drink from a clear mountain stream, you can both pick up giardia. Diarrhea and lethargy are the primary symptoms. Your veterinarian can test for giardia and prescribe treatment.

🦴 **Coccidiosis.** Coccidiosis is another parasitic protozoa, but this one is often carried by birds and rabbits. Symptoms include coughing, runny nose, eye discharge, or diarrhea. It can be diagnosed through a fecal analysis and your vet can prescribe treatment.

Yorkie Smarts

Take a sample of your Yorkie's feces to your veterinarian at least twice per year unless your vet requests it more often.

The Least You Need to Know

- As a general rule, Yorkies are healthy, although they can be affected by some genetic or congenital health problems.

- Vaccinations can prevent most of the diseases that threaten your Yorkie.

- Fleas and ticks are more than just pests; they can make your dog sick!

- Internal parasites are nasty and can threaten your dog's health.

Chapter 18

Preparing for Emergencies

In This Chapter

- ✷ Knowing where to get help
- ✷ Putting together an emergency first-aid kit
- ✷ Receiving emergency first-aid guidance
- ✷ Having disaster preparedness

I put together my first emergency first-aid kit almost 30 years ago. I was working at a veterinary hospital and saw a number of dogs come in, hurt, who had not even received basic first-aid care. In many situations, their owners could have saved their pets additional stress and harm simply by performing some basic first aid. I decided then that I would always have a first-aid kit available and I would know how to use the items in it. Since then, I've used my kit for myself and my husband, my own dogs, dogs belonging to friends and family, and even nieces and nephews! Friends and family make fun of my first-aid kit—a big red fishing tackle box—but they also know it's available and never hesitate to use it!

Emergencies do happen, unfortunately, and the best thing you can do is be prepared. Know what your veterinarian's emergency procedures are; have a credit card or cash ready; and know some basic first-aid techniques. Someday your dog's life could depend on it.

Know Where to Get Help

Some veterinarians don't handle after-hours emergencies; they refer their clients to emergency animal hospitals. Other vets take all calls no matter what the hour of day or night. Neither policy is right or wrong as long as you understand the policy and know whom to call when that *emergency* happens and have clear directions as to where to go.

Before an emergency occurs, ask your vet or the emergency animal clinic the following questions:

- **Where is the clinic located?** Can you find it easily? Make sure you can find it even when you might not be thinking clearly.

- **What are your policies regarding payment for emergency care?** Many require complete payment upon services. If that's so, can you pay it? What happens if an emergency happens between pay days? Some dog owners have gone to the trouble of obtaining a credit card (usually MasterCard or Visa because they're accepted just about anywhere) and they have saved that card for emergencies. That way it's never overextended and it's available for emergencies. If you have pet health insurance, make sure it covers emergencies and that the clinic will accept it.

Dog Talk

An **emergency** is considered to be a potentially life-threatening injury or illness; or a health threat that should not wait until the next day.

- **Do you have the facilities to keep dogs overnight? Does someone stay with the dog if he remains overnight?** Many times this depends on the situation, so ask for clarification for your own peace of mind.

- **If the dog spends the night, what happens during business hours?** Many emergency clinics are closed during business hours, so what will then happen? Will you be required to transport your dog to your veterinarian? Will the clinic do that?

- **Will the clinic forward the emergency information to my vet or should my vet call the clinic?** Or will you hand carry the records with your dog?

Yorkie Smarts

Don't wait until your dog is ill or injured to find out what your vet's emergency policies are. Ask now so you know.

Make sure your veterinarian's phone number and the number of the local emergency animal clinic are readily available. Post them on the refrigerator, and put them in your first-aid kit and in your wallet. Sometimes it's hard to think clearly in an emergency, so make things as easy for yourself as possible.

An Emergency First-Aid Kit

As I mentioned previously, I use a large fishing tackle box to hold all my supplies—I like how big it is and that it has a lot of little sections and boxes to hold small items. On the outside I have written in very large letters "First-Aid Kit." I want it to be easily seen so if I send someone to my van who doesn't know what the kit looks like, he or she can easily spot it.

Some supplies I keep in my kit—and suggest you keep in yours—include ...

- Large and small tweezers

- Round-ended scissors and pointed sharp scissors

- Disposable razors

- Small nail clippers (for small dogs or cats)

- Thermometer (rectal)

- Safety pins

- Mirror

- Pen and pencil

- Paper for notes and directions

- Tape of various sizes, widths, and types

- Butterfly adhesive bandages

- Rolls of gauze or fabric of different widths

- Gauze pads of different sizes, including eye pads

- Elastic wraparound bandages

- Instant cold compresses

- Antiseptic cleansing wipes

- Sterile saline eye wash

- Alcohol prep pads

- A small bottle of hydrogen peroxide

- Benadryl tablets

- Bactine

- Bacitracin ointment

- Kaopectate tablets or liquid

- A leash and collar

I also keep a gallon jug of water in my van, a dog bowl, and a couple of old towels.

You'll need to check this kit often, to replace materials that have been used and materials or medications that have expired. Most medications do have an expiration date; don't use them after that date.

If you don't know how to use these materials, consider enrolling in a first-aid class. The Red Cross offers a first-aid course for dog owners in many regions of the country. If that's not available in your area, veterinarians can often be convinced to teach a class for a dog club or group for a minimal charge.

Bet You Didn't Know

The Red Cross offers a class in canine first aid and CPR. Call the local branch of the Red Cross to find a course near you.

Restraining Your Yorkie

Hurt dogs often panic. They thrash, fight restraint, and bite, claw, or scratch at anyone who tries to touch them. Many dog owners are unpleasantly surprised when their wonderful, beloved dog bites them after an injury. An injured dog isn't thinking clearly and is concerned only with getting away from the hurt. You, then, need to know how to restrain your Yorkie so that he can be prevented from hurting himself more than he already has, and so that you can protect yourself.

Prevent Him from Biting

The first thing you need to learn how to do is to muzzle him. By closing his mouth, gently but firmly, you can make sure he doesn't bite anyone when he's afraid or hurt. Granted, Yorkies are very small, but they can bite quite hard when they want to and a hurt Yorkie can definitely hurt someone.

You can make a muzzle out of just about anything that is long and pliable. A leash works very well, as does a bandanna or a length of gauze from your first-aid kit. Take the length of leash

Watch Out!

Never muzzle a dog who is having trouble breathing!

or material and wrap it quickly around your dog's muzzle at least two times. Wrap it gently—a Yorkie's muzzle is very small—but firmly. Then pull the ends back behind your dog's ears and tie it behind the neck. If you gently pull on the material around the muzzle it shouldn't slip off.

Practice this on your Yorkie every once in a while. He won't like it, but that's okay. When you muzzle him, tell him what a good dog he is and when you take the muzzle off, give him a doggy treat to make up for the unpleasantness of it all!

To muzzle your Yorkie in an emergency, wrap the leash twice around his muzzle. Make sure he can still breathe.

Be Still in Your Arms

One of the nicest benefits to having a tiny dog is that it's much easier to restrain them in an emergency. A hurt Great Dane is tough to control; your Yorkie can be held in your arms!

Practice by picking up your Yorkie and rolling him over on his back so that he is resting on one of your forearms, his head toward the inside of your elbow. Your hand of that arm can cup his hips and his body can be cradled in your arm up against your body. Your other hand can rest on his chest, controlling him so that he doesn't thrash or fight you.

In this position, you can see his face and he can see yours—which should be calming for him. You can also look at him, examining him for injuries. When he calms, you can take the hand off his chest to help examine him through his coat.

Practice this position every once in a while so he doesn't resist it when you need to use it. When you do this, practice examining him in this position, too: touch his paws, look at his ears and teeth, and run your free hand through his coat. Let him get used to the whole examination. This way, in an emergency it won't be something completely new to him.

Canine CPR

Cardiopulmonary resuscitation (CPR) is a vital first-aid skill. I will never forget the day my husband Paul and I came upon a dog who had been hit by a car. There were only minor injuries apparent; however, the dog wasn't breathing. We began CPR and within a few minutes the dog began breathing again. After a trip to the emergency animal clinic and treatment (there were some internal injuries), the dog made a full recovery. For years afterward, every time we saw that dog, Paul and I felt good about our efforts.

With Yorkies, CPR is slightly different than for larger dogs because of their tiny size. First of all, when you see a Yorkie lying still, you should make a quick evaluation prior to doing anything. Take the following steps:

1. Lift the dog carefully, moving him as little as possible (in case of other injuries), to a table, bench, or chair.

2. Check whether there is a heartbeat by placing two fingertips under either armpit.

3. Check whether he's breathing. Watch for his chest to move, or wet a fingertip and place it in front of his nose. His breath can be felt on your wet fingertip.

4. If he's not breathing, clear his mouth of any obstructions.

> **Watch Out!**
>
> When doing CPR, you must compress the chest enough to move the blood in the heart, yet not so hard as to break your Yorkie's ribs! Perform the CPR firmly yet gently.

5. Pull the tongue out and to the side of his mouth so that it doesn't block the airway.

6. Close his mouth and pull his lips over the teeth to help make his mouth airtight. Cup your hand around his lips and muzzle.

7. Inhale a breath, and then exhale gently but firmly a small breath (a puff) into the dog's nose. Watch his chest for it to rise after you blow.

8. Repeat every five seconds if you can do so without hyperventilating yourself.

9. After 10 breaths, stop and do some chest compressions. Place him on his side, and using two fingers, compress the chest (very gently but enough to compress it slightly) five times. Then go back to giving him breaths. Do 10 breaths, then 5 chest compressions, then repeat the process.

> **Watch Out!**
>
> Don't practice CPR on a dog who isn't in a life-threatening situation. You could hurt him! Practice on a stuffed toy.

After you start CPR, continue it until your dog begins breathing again, until you can get your dog to help, or until it seems very obvious that it is in vain. But don't stop too soon, as many dogs have been saved by canine CPR.

Emergency First-Aid Guidelines

In an emergency situation, it's important to be able to think and react quickly. If your Yorkie is bleeding, in shock, or overheating, your quick reactions could mean the difference between life and death.

The emergency guidelines listed in the rest of this chapter are not given to replace veterinary care. Instead, they are to aid you in caring for your Yorkie until you can get him to appropriate emergency care.

Bet You Didn't Know

A small bag of frozen vegetables makes a great ice pack.

Bleeding

Bleeding occurs after just about any injury. How it should be treated depends on the type of bleeding and its severity. If the skin isn't broken, there may be bleeding under the skin. This can result in a bruise if the injury is small. A bruise can be treated with an ice pack. Use the ice pack on and off at 15-minute intervals until it seems that the bleeding under the skin has stopped.

Bleeding from small scrapes, scratches, and small cuts is usually not a danger. Wipe it off, apply pressure with a gauze pad if it's still oozing, and when the bleeding stops, gently wash it with soap and water.

Watch Out!

Yorkies are tiny and blood-loss can quickly lead to shock or cardiac arrest.

Internal bleeding is very dangerous and less obvious. If your Yorkie has been in some kind of a rough accident—especially if he has been kicked or dropped—watch his behavior. If he stops moving, acts restless, or cries, get him to the vet's office right away. Other symptoms of internal bleeding include pale gums, a distended abdomen, bloody diarrhea, bloody vomit, blood in the saliva, or coughed-up blood.

A continuous oozing type of bleeding is also serious. You will need to put pressure on the wound, using layers of gauze pads and pressure from your hand, and you'll want to get the dog to your veterinarian right away. Stitches will probably be required.

Shock

A dog (like a person) will go into shock after a traumatic injury or during a serious, sudden illness. Shock is life-threatening and, when combined with what caused the shock in the first place, your dog could be in serious danger of dying.

Symptoms of shock include …

❧ A rise in heart rate, often irregular

❧ Panting or very rapid breathing; often gasping

❧ Dilated pupils; a staring, glazed look to the eyes; pale gums; and no response to movement

> **Watch Out!**
> Never leave your dog alone in the car. The air inside a car heats up very quickly, even on cool days, and your dog could die of heatstroke before you return.

You cannot treat your Yorkie for shock, other than keeping him warm, keeping him still, and getting him to a veterinarian right away. This is not the time to watch the dog and hope he'll come out of it on his own; he needs help right away!

Heatstroke

A dog who is overheating will lay down, often flopping himself down, or will pace back and forth in agitation. He will be panting heavily and may go into shock. His body temperature will rise rapidly. You will need to immediately cool him down. Immerse him in cool water or pack him in ice and immediately get him to the vet's office.

Poisons

Symptoms of poisoning can vary depending on what caused it. Some of the more common symptoms include extreme salivation and drooling, vomiting, diarrhea, and muscle tremors. The puppy's eyes may be dilated or he may suffer seizures.

In all situations where you suspect your Yorkie may be poisoned, call your veterinarian. Listed below are some of the more common household substances that are harmful to your puppy and what you should do if your puppy gets into them:

- **Antifreeze.** Induce vomiting and get your puppy to the vet's office right away.

- **Bleach.** Call your vet right away. He may ask you to induce vomiting or may recommend your bring your Yorkie to his office immediately.

- **Chocolate.** This is poisonous to dogs, so make him vomit and then call your vet.

- **Gasoline.** Give him some vegetable oil to block absorption and take him to the vet's office right away.

- **Ibuprofen.** Make him vomit and get him to the vet's office right away.

- **Insecticides.** If ingested, get him to the vet right away. Do not induce vomiting unless your vet recommends it. If there was skin contact, wash him thoroughly.

- **Rat, mouse, roach, or snail poisons.** Induce vomiting and get him to your vet's office right away.

> **? Bet You Didn't Know**
>
> You can get your Yorkie to vomit by giving him a teaspoon of hydrogen peroxide. If he doesn't throw up within five minutes, give him another teaspoon. After five more minutes, give him one more. If he still hasn't thrown up, call your veterinarian again.

> **Yorkie Smarts**
>
> The National Poison Control Center 24-hour poison hotline is 1-900-680-0000. No credit card is needed; your phone bill will be charged.

Bring with you to your vet's office whatever it was your Yorkie got into. If at all possible, bring the label with the name of the product and any ingredients. The more information you can give your vet, the better.

Burns

Burns can happen in a variety of ways. Thermal burns are those caused by heat, such as if your dog gets too close to a candle. Electrical burns can occur when the dog chews on an electrical cord. Chemical burns are the result of contact with a corrosive substance that causes a burn, such as bleach, gasoline, liquid drain cleaners, paint thinners, or road salt.

If you suspect your Yorkie has been burned, follow these directions:

1. If the burn is chemical in nature, rinse your Yorkie thoroughly. Treat it also as a potential poisoning.

2. Put an ice pack on the spot.

3. If the burn is not severe and the skin is simply red, keep it clean and watch it carefully to make sure it doesn't get infected.

4. If the burn is blistered, bleeding, and oozing or has damaged any layers of skin, take your Yorkie to the vet's office right away.

Insect Bites and Stings

If you suspect your dog has been stung or bitten by an insect, first try to find where on your dog's body the bite or sting happened. If there is a stinger, scrape it out. Don't grab it and pull it; that will squeeze more venom into your dog's skin. Scrape it out with a fingernail.

If you need to, shave away some of the dog's hair so you can see the sting or bite. Wash the area off, pour some hydrogen peroxide on it, and watch it. Some signs of allergic reaction include the following:

- Swelling at the site of the bite or sting and in the body tissues surrounding it
- Redness or extreme whiteness
- Fever

🦴 Muscle ache, joint pain, and lameness

🦴 Vomiting and/or diarrhea

🦴 Difficulty breathing

If your dog is showing any of these allergic reactions, call your veterinarian right away. Your vet may recommend that you give your dog a Benadryl antihistamine immediately to combat some of the allergic reaction. He will also want to see your Yorkie as soon as you can bring him in.

Animal Bites

If your Yorkie is bitten by another small dog during playtime and the bite is a simple puncture, don't be too worried. Simply wash the bite and watch it. If it looks red and possibly infected, call your veterinarian. Check with the owner of the other dog to make sure the dog is well vaccinated, including for rabies.

However, if your Yorkie is attacked by a much larger dog, or an unknown dog, call your vet immediately, as this could pose a serious health threat. If you can, try to find the dog's owner to make sure the dog is vaccinated, especially with an up-to-date rabies vaccine. Some bites may need special treatment, including antibiotics, drains, or stitches, to make sure they heal properly. There is also the danger that a larger dog could have caused internal injuries to your Yorkie.

Watch Out!
Wild animals carrying the rabies virus are not that uncommon. Skunks, raccoons, bats, and foxes have all been known to carry it. The best prevention is to make sure your Yorkie is vaccinated.

If your dog is bitten by a cat or a wild animal, you must get him to the veterinarian's office right away. Cat bites must be cleaned thoroughly right away as infections afterward are very common. Bites from wild animals must also be treated, and there is the very real danger of rabies.

Snake Bite

If your Yorkie is bitten by a nonvenomous snake, wash the wound with hydrogen peroxide or chlorhexidine and watch it to make sure the wound doesn't get infected.

If your Yorkie is bitten by a venomous snake, don't panic. First of all, many snakes do not automatically inject venom; the snake may strike to scare away your dog without actually injecting venom.

If venom is injected, your dog will begin to swell. If he was bitten on the leg, the leg will swell. Unfortunately, most dogs are bitten on the face because they stick their nose down into the snake's space and *whap!* the snake gets the dog on the nose or muzzle. If the nose or muzzle begins to swell, the dog is in great danger of suffocating, so get him to the veterinarian's office right away. Call ahead so the vet can begin making arrangements immediately to get the anti-venom. Take a good look at the snake so you can describe it to your vet; not all snakes are venomous.

While getting him to the vet's office, you need to stay calm so you can keep your dog calm. Keep him quiet, too, because limited movement will aid in slowing down the spread of the venom in his system.

Natural (and Other) Disasters

Where do you live? In Southern California, we must deal with wild-fires and earthquakes. In the Midwest, dog owners must put up with tornadoes. Florida residents must be able to survive hurricanes. Natural disasters—no matter where you live—are a fact of life, and you need to make preparations so that you can take care of your Yorkie as well as your family.

I keep my canine first-aid kit (which is combined with human first-aid supplies) easily accessible. When on vacation or a trip, the first-aid kit is in my van. I also have on hand a gallon jug of water; more when we're traveling in the desert. Extra leashes and collars are always in my van as well as in the first-aid kit.

In my garage, within reach of the side door, I keep an emergency kit in case of earthquakes or fires. This is a trashcan with wheels on the bottom so I can easily move it. I keep both supplies for my husband and myself as well as supplies for our dogs and cats in this kit.

For the dogs I have the following:

- Veterinary records, including shot records, and the vet's phone number.

Yorkie Smarts

My dogs always wear a buckle collar with an identification tag with my name and phone number on it as well as their license tag. My dogs are also tattooed and microchipped for identification.

- If any of the dogs need medication, I keep some on hand.

- Dog food, including canned food that will store for quite a while, as well as canned meats and rice.

- A can opener.

- An emergency first-aid kit.

- Grooming supplies; the Yorkie's coat cannot be ignored.

- Toys and chewies to keep your dog amused.

- Extra leashes and collars.

I also have dog crates easily accessible and make sure I always have enough crates for all our pets. The crates are taken apart and stacked in the garage near the emergency kit.

A few of my neighbors think I'm either a little neurotic or overly concerned, but my husband and I have lived in this area for many years and three times have been evacuated due to wildfires. When ordered to evacuate, you don't have time to put stuff together. You grab what you can and leave. My emergency kit and the extra crates have come in handy and they are there for any future emergencies.

Think about emergencies you may have to face in your region. If you live in a cold climate, make sure there are blankets and chemical hand warmers in your emergency kit. In a hot region you may want some extra water.

Last but not least, in a disaster, never leave your Yorkie behind when you evacuate. It's a federal law now that evacuation shelters must make plans for pets, so bring your pets with you—with your emergency kit and the dog's crate. As we saw after Hurricane Katrina and other disasters, pets left home alone are vulnerable and far too many die. Make plans now and then take your pets with you.

The Least You Need to Know

- Know where to get help in an emergency; both from your veterinarian and the local emergency animal clinic.

- Know how to restrain your Yorkie in an emergency so you can keep him from harm and protect yourself.

- Put together a first-aid kit, and keep it stocked and handy.

- Make plans for disasters and emergencies before they happen.

Yorkies (and Other Dogs) on the Internet

The Internet is a wonderful research tool for all dog owners. Yorkie owners can find some enriching sites on the Internet. If you're looking for Yorkie breeders, Yorkie jewelry, books on Yorkies, or Yorkie clubs, you can find them all on the Internet.

Be cautious, however. Never assume that everything you read on the Internet is correct. Anyone can post a web page, and while there is good information out there, there's also a lot of garbage! Don't hesitate to ask questions, and always look into who is doing the writing.

Yorkie-Specific Sites

Kritters in the Mailbox—Yorkie gifts: www.krittersinthemailbox.com

United Yorkie Rescue—Rescue and adoption group: www.unitedyorkierescue.org

Yorkie Haven Rescue—Rescue and adoption group: www.yorkiehavenrescue.com

Yorkie Rescue Me—Rescue and adoption group: www.yorkierescueme.com

Yorkshire Terrier Club of America, Inc.: www.ytca.org

Yorkshire Terrier National Rescue, Inc.: www.yorkierescue.com

Health

Nutrition Navigator: www.navigator.tufts.edu

The Pfizer Animal Health website: www.petnet.com

Veterinary Pet Insurance: www.petinsurance.com

General and Miscellaneous Information

Amazon online bookstore: www.amazon.com

Dog Owner's Guide: www.canismajor.com/dog/guide

Dogwise dog books: www.dogwise.com

J and J Dog Supplies: www.jandjdog.com

J-B Wholesale Pet Supplies, Inc.: www.jbpet.com

Dog Sports

American Kennel Club: www.akc.org

American Working Terrier Association: www.dirt-dog.com

Association of Pet Dog Trainers: www.apdt.com

Canine Freestyle Federation, Inc.: www.canine-freestyle.org

Canine Performance Events, Inc.: www.k9cpe.com

The Foundation for Pet-Provided Therapy: www.loveonaleash.org

Musical Dog Sport Association: www.musicaldogsport.org

North American Dog Agility Council: www.nadac.com

North American Flyball Association: www.flyball.org

Therapy Dogs Inc.: www.therapydogs.com

United Kennel Club: www.ukcdogs.com

United States Dog Agility Association: www.usdaa.com

The World Canine Freestyle Organization: www.worldcaninefreestyle.org

Index